REINVENTING YOURSELF

Overcome your anxiety and fear

when faced with life's

problems and challenges

MARIO ALONSO PUIG

MJF BOOKS
NEW YORK

Published by MJF Books
Fine Communications
322 Eighth Avenue
New York, NY 10001

Reinventing Yourself
LC Control Number: 2013948079
ISBN 978-1-60671-218-4

Page design: Rajdip Sanghera

This edition is published by MJF Books in arrangement with Marshall Cavendish
Editions, an imprint of Marshall Cavendish International.

The author and publishers have used their best efforts in preparing this book and disclaim
liability arising directly and indirectly from the use and application of this book.

All reasonable efforts have been made to obtain necessary copyright permissions. Any
omissions or errors are unintentional and will, if brought to the attention of the publishers,
be corrected in future printings.

Printed in the United States of America.

MJF Books and the MJF colophon are trademarks of Fine Creative Media, Inc.

QF   10   9   8   7   6   5   4   3   2

For my wife, Isabella, and my three sons, Mario, Joaquin and Borja, for being lovely individuals who inspire me every day and help me to be a little better. You are my true masters and the biggest motivation which helps me to get over the fear of overcoming my own limitations.

For my mother, Maria Celia, somebody full of beauty, courage, commitment and love for life. A never-ending inspiration and an example of a person who can overcome anything.

For my five brothers, Jose Maria, Manuel, Juan Ignacio, Fernando and Alejandro. I will always feel an infinite gratitude for the great luck of having found you on my path.

To the memory of my father who will always remain in my heart as someone who tried to give me the roots to grow from and wings to fly.

To the memory of Joaquin, someone I shall never forget.

CONTENTS

"In our naivety we have forgotten that beneath our world of reason another one lies buried."

CARL GUSTAV JUNG

INTRODUCTION

We have all faced obstacles and problems in life which have often brought us to a standstill. It's as if we have been invaded with a profound conviction that the problem cannot be sorted out or, simply, that we do not have the talent or the necessary ability to find a solution.

Many people do not know what to do when their relationship with another person is not as they would like it to be. Others would like to be more daring, more decisive, to learn a new sport, a foreign language or simply to understand how to work a computer better. But something gets in the way and they finally decide to give up. There are human beings that wish to feel appreciated a little bit more, to strengthen their self-esteem, so that others respect them. In the end, after a series of failed attempts, they end up giving in.

Nowadays, there are also people who have experienced one failure after another and feel unable to keep going. They are individuals who have done everything within their reach to keep their companies, their work, their families and their lives up and running. They feel that all this effort has not been worth it, that at heart it has been a complete waste of time. I have written this book for all these people because their suffering is not foreign to me.

I have spent many years of my life trying to understand the complexity found in every one of us and the curious reactions that we have when we are faced with adverse circumstances. My research started out with a simple question: When faced with certain challenges, what is it that clouds our mind and makes us unable to think clearly, while at the same time all our energy is drained and we experience that funny feeling in our stomach?

> *"Anxiety is a curious state of uneasiness because we start to suffer in the present for something that we do not even know for sure is going to happen in the future."*

Anxiety levels are continually increasing throughout the world as people are confronted with constant and profound changes and doubts in their lives. The formula for generating an anxious state in human beings is really simple. You only have to imagine that in the future a series of problems will appear and that we are going to be unable to solve them. Anxiety is a curious state of uneasiness because we start to suffer in the present for something that we do not even know for sure is going to happen in the future. René Descartes, the great 17th-century French mathematician and philosopher, wrote a letter at the end of his life from which this original comment is taken:

"My life has been full of misfortunes, many of which never took place".

"If we wish to increase our capacity to solve problems [...], we need to learn how to transcend the limits that our mind has set us."

We need to see what is hidden in the depths of our mind, because only then will we be able to understand clearly where exactly our real limitations lie. We will not find the answer to this state of mind by thinking things over and over again in our bewildered minds, but rather by looking in a very different place. As Albert Einstein put it, "No problem can be solved from the same level of consciousness that created it."

If the mind has such an ability to let worry take root, how are we going to be able to solve this situation by using the same method that created the problem in the first place? If we wish to increase our capacity to solve problems and become more competent when looking for opportunities, we need to learn how to transcend the limits that our mind has set us.

In this book we are going to spend time looking at many of the least known, but most important, aspects of how the human brain works. I am completely confident that, when you understand why we act as we do, you will then be able to start planning new strategies which will allow you to obtain what, until now, seemed out of your reach.

Training schemes in general attach great value to erudition and, indeed, this is what they evaluate. However, they neither grade nor measure in any way the abilities and virtues of listening, empathy, self-knowledge, wisdom, leadership, courage, compassion or others which later often make for success in life.

This book is an inward journey because some of the resources that we most need in order to face the challenges which life presents to us can only be found within ourselves.

Personal change is not about knowledge or erudition but about motivation. It is only people who feel truly motivated who will make the necessary effort to bring into flower what has remained hidden and unexplored within them.

I invite you to walk with me on this road of self-discovery, in which we will progressively learn that what is within us, is a magical and surprising realm. When we delve a little bit further into our real selves we will realize that much of the anxiety and suffering we feel in life is optional and that our basic nature is a source of Energy, Wisdom, Serenity, Joy, Creativity and Love.

MARIO ALONSO PUIG

1. REINVENT YOURSELF

"It isn't the strongest species which survives,
neither the most intelligent, but rather that which
adapts best to change."

CHARLES DARWIN

One of the hardest things to do is to be open-minded when you are exploring ideas that challenge your usual way of thinking. We all know that what our brain is capable of perceiving is only a small part of what reality entails. However, the moment we wish to act, we tend to do so as if what we see is the only thing that exists. For example, how often does the well-trained eye fail to make out colours and shapes instantly but can recognize what people are feeling. There are areas of reality which, if we were to reach them, would reveal many things which would help us live longer and a better quality of life. It is logical that we ask ourselves why this strange situation has arisen which makes us so blind to and unaware of those life opportunities which are before us.

It's only by understanding a little more about the interaction between the mind and the brain that we can find an explanation as to why the brain doesn't work at the level of efficiency that we would expect it to. We often hear that we only use 10% of our brain. This statement has no scientific base, and even if it had, we all know in some intuitive way that we have resources, strengths and talent within ourselves which are still to be discovered.

The brain is such a complex organ that, despite only weighing 2% of our body weight, it consumes 25% of our blood. Processes such as analysis, learning or creative thinking require a great deal of energy which comes in the form of glucose and oxygen through the blood. The most important mission that the brain has is to help us to survive.

> *" The brain is such a complex organ that, despite only weighing 2% of our body weight, it consumes 25% of our blood. "*

More than two million years ago, homo habilis survived whilst his cousins, the parantropos did not. The reason is simply that the first of the two developed a bigger and more efficient brain.

The task of surviving has a lot to do with the capacity to solve problems, make decisions, face challenges and learn from our mistakes. Our ability to observe and analyse, combined with intelligence, memory, imagination and creativity, make up the foundations we need in order to face life's challenges efficiently. That said, all of these abilities and faculties are pretty much useless if we get overcome with anxiety and worry when we come face-to-face with our challenges.

Whether we like it or not, someone who is overcome with emotions is intellectually at a dead-end.

The emotions we feel and which have such importance when we come to try to solve problems, do not come out of a void but rather have a clear and specific root. Knowing the origins of these emotions is very important if we wish to manage them effectively. This is particularly true when we find ourselves in a tricky situation, where we are put under a lot of pressure and where our decisions can have important consequences.

When feelings like fear or desperation take hold of us we experience a kind of "brain kidnapping", and however intelligent we may be, our intelligence will not be found anywhere. What makes most of our problems unsolvable is not the difficulty of the problem but rather the feeling we get that we are not up to the challenge the moment we face them. For this reason, the true capacity to solve problems in a creative way lies in keeping a sufficient mental balance when these problems arise, so that we can react in the best possible way and find an efficient solution.

From metallurgy we have adopted the word *resilience*, which basically refers to the resistance that a metal has to being deformed. We have also adopted the word *elasticity* from the same science, which is the capacity of a metal to return to its original form when the force that has deformed it has disappeared. Steel, for example, has great resistance as it is very difficult to deform it and it also has great elasticity to return to its original shape once the force that has acted on it has gone.

There are people who have an extraordinary capacity to put up with adversity and who rarely lose their patience. It tends to be these same people who overcome a painful episode in their lives quicker.

We have coined the word *homeostasis* from medicine, which refers to the group of mechanisms which stabilizes internal physiological conditions. We are keen to learn how to develop this resilience and this elasticity within ourselves. We are interested in finding out how to develop these mechanisms to hold on to our homeostasis, our balanced state, when we find ourselves in difficult and even adverse circumstances. To achieve such competence, it is necessary to look into the complex springs of the human mind with the aim of discovering how to manage them in the best possible way.

Even though I do not like the analogy between the human brain and the computer, it is nevertheless useful in order to understand certain slippery notions. Our brain is rather like a sophisticated computer which is able to carry out the most challenging calculations and to find the most innovative solutions. Nevertheless, just as a computer works with a software program, our brain also functions with a kind of software located within it. A wonderful computer using poor software generates poor results. An exceptional brain functioning with limited mental software will only produce limited operations.

> **"**Our mental software is basically built up of experiences.**"**

Our mental software is basically built up of experiences. These experiences become the reference points which decide the way the brain has to work in the future. Let's imagine, for example, that someone has had a series of very negative experiences with a person of the opposite sex as a boss. The consequence of that would be, if that person has a boss of the opposite gender in his next job, he would most likely begin to feel some very unpleasant feelings. These perhaps would be frustration, resentment or even anger. The performance of this individual could be poor, by being absent-minded and making many mistakes in his work. This would be a clear case of a perfectly capable brain made unable to cope due to experiential software that is continually imposing limits on him.

Something similar could happen to a child who has experienced a lot of suffering when learning something new. When pushed into new learning experiences, the child will be unable to hold his attention, and to understand and memorize things.

Parts of the experiences we have built up throughout our lives are essential for survival and, therefore, are where they should be. Nevertheless, other experiences are, as we have seen, deeply limiting, and they impede our ability to adapt to unstable and changing circumstances. It is precisely these kinds of experiences which we most need to know about and understand because, when we change them, our brain also changes and becomes more capable.

The software cannot damage the hardware (the physical structure of the computer) except if it has caught some kind of computer virus. However, the mental software, when it is dysfunctional, can harm the physical hardware of the brain. For this reason, if we change a dysfunctional mental program for one that works well, this does indeed produce a clear improvement in the physical structure of the human brain.

It is generally accepted that the adult brain is malleable. We now know that, changing the way we think, changes the neural networks. We also know that people trapped in a negative frame of mind favour the death of neurons, and those of us that have decided to think positively, give birth to new neurons from stem cells in the brain.

> *"Mental software, when it is dysfunctional, can do harm to the physical body, the hardware in the brain."*

When we change our most limiting mental programs for others which are less so, we physically modify the structure of our brains. Perhaps it was for this reason that Dr. Santiago Ramón y Cajal, the first winner of the Nobel Prize for Medicine (in 1906), declared that every human being can be, if he so wishes, the sculptor of his own brain. It is important to realize that Cajal was not speaking metaphorically but literally. This should make those of us who aspire to grow and develop our intelligence and our capacity for learning very joyful. But it also puts into our hands a great responsibility – that of discovering what we need to do, and how to train ourselves, to reinvent ourselves.

A FINAL WORD

If you wish to reinvent yourself,
focus on what you wish for and
not on what you fear.

2. LOOKING INSIDE YOURSELF

"Who is able to make dirty water clean?
Leave it be and little by little it will become clear."

LAO TZU

Our experiences, when they have been intense from an emotional point of view and, above all, if they took place during our childhood, can give rise to what is known as "unconscious beliefs". Such beliefs are in fact convictions that we have. We are dealing with feelings of certainty and therefore they cannot be debated. They are not like ideas, but rather are true feelings. It is very different to think, for example, that I am not capable of doing something, than to feel myself unable to do it. When we speak of these beliefs we are speaking of something that is deeply rooted in our minds. I would like to highlight here the fact that most of the convictions which limit us do so without us even being aware of them. That is, they act in our subconscious mind.

Many of us have probably heard of the intelligence quotient test which, for years, was considered able to measure the intelligence of a person. When a group of young people were helped to uncover some of those deeply limiting convictions they had about who they were (and to transform them into more positive convictions), their intellectual quotients were increased by an extraordinary degree. This basically means that some of our convictions can limit our intellectual development in a significant way.

"Most of the convictions which limit us do so without us even being aware of them. That is, they act in our subconscious mind."

Very often we are convinced that we are made a certain way and we feel it is impossible to transform ourselves. However, I state again that what our brain is capable of recognizing and understanding about ourselves is only a small part of the reality when it comes to who we are. Indeed, it is convenient to know that our brain, in terms of perception, can completely mislead us.

When you observe a sunrise and follow the movement of the sun until it disappears from sight, the visual perception that one has is that the sun has moved, while you have stayed still. It was very difficult for Galileo to open the minds of people to an idea that was in complete opposition, not only to what they thought, but also to what they saw.

There are a series of ideas that we tend to ignore from the start because they contradict what our five senses show us. I'll give you another example to make the point clearer. We all understand that matter is made up of atoms and since our body is composed of matter, it is also made up of atoms. When we look at our body, we perceive it as something solid, yet this is a perception which does not tally with reality.

On one occasion I visited the Science Museum in London and I was explained something surprising. The part of an atom which we can call "solid" is the nucleus which, if we recall some of our physics lessons, is surrounded by an empty cortex where the electrons are in motion. So, to get an idea of just how empty an atom is, the nucleus would be the size of a football placed in the centre of London, whilst the surrounding cortex would take up all of London, whose diameter would be about 50 kilometres. If we are formed of atoms, as indeed we are, that means we are basically empty, even though we see ourselves as solid matter.

Our visceral being changes so much that many of the organs that we have now do not have any of the cells we had when we were born. They are new cells that have appeared as a consequence of the process of cellular reproduction that is going on in the body all the time.

"If we do not change our limited way of thinking we will be unable to see things from a perspective which allows us to discover doors where before we only saw walls."

You will need to be very open-minded when you read the pages that follow. Extraordinary events are not going to be revealed but rather we are going to realize that if we do not change our limited way of thinking we will be unable to see things from a perspective which allows us to discover doors where before we only saw walls. We need to recover that sense of wonder and surprise we had as children so as to enter what Einstein called "the beauty of mystery".

We became aware of the existence of micro-organisms thanks to the invention of an observation tool called the microscope and we became aware of the reality of galaxies through the use of the telescope. We are going to need a very special tool to enter ourselves and discover that which, although existing, remains hidden from view. This observation tool is none other than self-awareness.

I would now like to recount to you a fascinating story told to me by Stephen Covey:

Two fishermen were fishing on a river in the United States, using the fly technique. This was made popular by many movies and involves the fishing line moving like a whip over the water, occasionally striking the surface of the water so as to give the impression that an insect had fallen into it. This immediately makes the trout rise up to the bait. Logically, for the fish to have time to catch the bait, it has to feel it is close to it. For this reason it is very important for the bait to touch the water close to the fish.

One of these fishermen caught loads of fish while the other didn't manage to catch any at all. When asked about the possible explanation for this curious situation, many people mentioned luck and others, experience. Reality is far removed from what may seem most likely. The fisherman who caught so many fish wore special glasses called "polarized glasses" and these enabled him to make out the silhouette of the fishes below the surface of the water. Those of us who are not especially keen on fishing would never have guessed that this was the explanation, as we wouldn't have imagined that there were glasses capable of such a feat.

Our consciousness is rather like the polarized glasses of this story. That is what will help us to discover what is within ourselves. That which doesn't allow us to live life as we'd like to in those areas which depend on our own judgement, and there are many.

Consciousness needs attention. It is like the eye that sees. Attention is like the light that shines so that the eye can see. Only when we pay attention to our inner self can we discover that which had remained covered over and reveal that which was veiled.

A FINAL WORD

Beneath many of one's deepest
fears, there isn't a real inability
to face them, but rather the
belief that one is unable
to do so.

3. TWO MINDS IN ONE HEAD

"The first person singular – that little devil called me – is not first, nor a person, nor singular."

JAMES HILLMAN

In the 1930s there was a mental disorder for which no cure existed. It generally affected children and the young and it often caused serious injuries, and even death. It was a strange illness named epilepsy. When a group of brain cells generally found close to a small scar located in the cerebral cortex got disturbed, they began producing a series of sudden, excessive electric shocks. These shocks, rather like a wave that extends across the surface of a lake, went on to affect the group of neurons located in the area which also sent out electric charges. When these electric charges reached the corpus callosum, one of the bridges connecting the two sides of the brain, the whole brain then found itself in that abnormal state and the person went through what is known as an epileptic state. The sick person lost consciousness, fell to the floor and began to have convulsions. Sometimes, he fell over a fireplace or on a hard floor, which explained why there were dramatic consequences at times. Another problem was that, in the convulsive state, the person could suffocate and die as a result. The doctors didn't know what to do to solve this mental disorder. At that time neuropharmacology was in its early days and all the alternative therapies that can be so efficient in treating this malady successfully today were simply not available then.

It was the brain surgeons of the time that decided to come up with a risky solution. They knew that the epileptic discharge began in one particular area of the brain and that the symptoms and signs the patient presented could lead them towards where the first discharge had taken place. They named this constellation of symptoms and signs the epileptic aura. If, for example, the initial focus was located in an area connected with vision, the patient noted flashes of light. If it was in the temporal lobe, he could hear sounds and even experience hallucinations.

The surgeons thought that if they could stop the electrical discharge from passing from one brain hemisphere to the other, they could at least prevent the patient entering that feared epileptic state. What the brain surgeons were suggesting was alarming, as it involved cutting into the corpus callosum, a structure which has more than 500 million nerve fibres. What would happen to a human being whose two brain hemispheres were not able to be in contact with each other? Would the remedy perhaps be worse than the sickness?

As they couldn't see any other alternative on the horizon, the doctors decided to go ahead with the experiment, and to this end they made use of monkeys, which have always been of such help in medical research. Once anaesthetized and the cranium opened, they began the meticulous sectioning of the bridge linking the two hemispheres. Then they took the monkeys to a post-operation ward to observe what would happen when these monkeys woke up.

The scientists were astounded when they saw that the cutting of the corpus callosum in the monkeys didn't appear to have any negative effects on them. Motivated by these findings, they then looked at human beings who suffered this illness. Of course the difference between a monkey and a human being is great, and this explains why in the first operations, the brain surgeons only dared to make incomplete cuts of the corpus callosum. This resulted in the epileptic charge finding it harder to find the bridge to jump across to the other hemisphere as only part of it existed. Still, it managed to do so and in that moment a new epileptic state was unleashed. In some way, the solution of partially cutting the corpus callosum only postponed the manifestation of the symptoms. But the scientists were in high spirits as those patients that had had their corpus callosum partially sectioned didn't seem to have any post-surgery second effects. The doctors went on to completely cut the corpus callosum. The result was extraordinary as this time the epileptic discharge could not reach the other hemisphere and, just as with the monkeys, the total sectioning of the corpus callosum did not appear to have any negative second effects. From that moment on, it was generally recognized that the corpus callosum was a structure that one could disregard.

For many years, nothing changed until the scientist Roger Sperry appeared on the scene. He got interested in the so-called "Californian divided brain series". This series covered those patients that years before had had their corpus callosum sectioned. Many of them, who were children at the time, were now adults leading completely normal lives.

Sperry asked a series of questions: How was it possible that you can cut a structure of such proportions without the brain noting it? How can one side of the brain be aware of what is happening in the other side if it can't communicate with it? This, without a doubt, led him to keep looking until he worked out the enigma, which earned him the Nobel Prize for Medicine and Physiology in 1981.

What this researcher found out at the Californian Institute of Technology was much more than an explanation as to why the patients had not experienced any deficit after the sectioning of the corpus callosum. Roger Sperry discovered something so fascinating and surprising that even today we find it hard to fully understand.

Allow me, dear reader, to explain one or two things about the way the brain works so that you can understand the foundations of Professor Sperry's findings and see the importance they have in our lives. If one looks straight ahead, everything seen by our left field of vision will be perceived by our right brain hemisphere. Everything located in our right side field of vision will be perceived by our left brain hemisphere. However, what we hear on our left side will go to both sides of the brain and the same is true of what we hear on our right side. On the other hand, the right half of our body is controlled by the left brain hemisphere and the left half of our body by the right. So, if we know someone who has had brain damage on his left hemisphere we will see that the area that he finds difficult to move will be the right area of the body.

If I project an image onto a screen for someone in such a way that he can only see it with his left brain hemisphere (by projecting it on his right visual field), and if I also ensure that this person cannot move his, unless his corpus callosum is intact, his right brain hemisphere will have no idea what he is seeing.

Sperry invented a type of lens which did not allow each brain area to have access to the visual field which did not correspond. Then, in the case of men, amongst other images projected was one with some naked women. These images were projected in such a way that they could only be registered by the left brain hemisphere. As these same people had had their corpus callosum sectioned, the data could not pass to the other side of the brain.

"What can you see?" asked Sperry.

"Some naked women, Professor."

There was something strange in their answers because they didn't reveal any emotion in their descriptions. Besides this, their skin did not manifest any galvanic reaction either. The galvanic reaction of the skin is what lie detectors focused on as it is an involuntary reaction which comes about when something produces an affective discharge in us.

Later Sperry projected the word *mother* on the same screen. The male patients could work out its meaning without any difficulty. However, they displayed no emotion in their descriptions.

So Sperry changed the position of the screen and projected the images of the naked women in such a way that only the right brain hemisphere of these patients could perceive it and that is when something curious happened. The men started to go red in the face and get nervous while the galvanic reaction in their skin made evident a clear emotional impact. Then Sperry asked them what had occurred.

Most people only have language areas in the left brain hemisphere. This implies that we have to respond to questions from this side. Nevertheless, the men could not answer Sperry because their left brain hemispheres hadn't seen the images and therefore their typical answer was none other than, "Professor, it is very hot in this room and you are making us a bit nervous".

It is true that their left brain hemispheres couldn't see the images of the naked women, but they could still perceive the intense changes that had taken place within their bodies and the way they had interpreted this was by attributing it to an apparent heat and to Sperry.

The conclusion that Sperry came to was that human beings not only have two brain hemispheres but, moreover, have two minds that process reality in a different way, and each complementing the other. Both minds therefore must have two distinct consciousnesses, allowing us to be aware of different aspects of the world.

The left brain hemisphere is the expert when it comes to analysing and storing data. We couldn't learn new ideas and new concepts if we did not possess a left brain hemisphere. It carries out a key function when we have to learn new routines and look for solutions. In this way we can respond in an effective and practical way to many of the challenges that we have to face. Without a left hemisphere we wouldn't have any capacity for using numbers or letters. They would have no meaning for us. Besides, we would find it very hard to identify the parts of a whole. The left hemisphere is the hemisphere of knowledge and scholarship which is something to which our society attaches great value.

> "*Sperry's conclusion is that human beings not only have two brain hemispheres but also two minds [...]. Both minds therefore must have two distinct consciousnesses.*"

The right hemisphere functions in a much more subtle way. It is a great expert in spatial tasks. It is the source of imagination and, therefore, is a key player in the creative process. The right hemisphere, in contrast to the left, works laterally, processing millions of bits of data simultaneously. Its great talent is not to be found in the analysis of the different elements of something but rather in working out the relationships which bind these elements together. Besides this, it has a much more intense connection than the left brain hemisphere with the limbic system which is our emotional brain centre. For this reason, Sperry's patients only showed such emotivism when the images were presented to the right brain hemisphere and not to the left. The right brain is especially active during sleep and in diverse meditation techniques. (Although in certain forms of meditation, there is a very intense increase in the activity of the prefrontal cortex of the left brain. This area has a very important role in the generation of positive emotions like joy and compassion.) Today we know that the right brain hemisphere is much more alert to what is happening in our bodies than the left brain hemisphere, especially in regard to our alarm system when we are presented with a possible danger. The right brain hemisphere is the most important when we have to deal with a new and unfamiliar environment. We can even see this increase in right brain activity in animals when they are faced with uncertain situations. The reason could be that the stereotyped conduct that is managed from the left brain hemisphere can be very useful when we move calmly about in our comfort area but not when our environment has been changed and we don't know where we are. We need to bear in mind that the right brain is receiving a lot of data from our surroundings without us being aware of it. Also, it is connecting this data with the information it already has, and all this activity has just one aim, which is to discover the patterns that are operating in this new environment. Once strategies have been discovered and developed to aid a smooth transition, this new operating strategy will be stored away in the left brain hemisphere.

One of the key differences between both hemispheres is how they transmit data to us to make us aware of it. The left hemisphere uses thought in the form of words, while the right brain hemisphere which lacks language centres, has to deal with information in a different way. It communicates this through body sensations, images, symbols and emotions. This is one of the big problems: we pay too much attention to what we think and hardly any to the feelings we have and to which we could broadly describe as intuition.

You may recall that it was epilepsy which helped Roger Sperry to decipher some of the most surprising capacities that both brain hemispheres have. We have gone a long way since that time and, for example, now know that the left brain hemisphere acts as a kind of inhibitor over the right hemisphere. We also know that the right brain hemisphere is the door to the unconscious and to a completely different perception of reality to that which we have when it is the left hemisphere which dominates our lives.

On 10 December 1996, an extraordinary woman, an American neuro-anatomist called Jill Taylor, experienced an ictus, a cerebrovascular accident on rupturing an arteriovenous malformation on the surface of her left brain hemisphere. This type of congenital malformation forms a ball of blood vessels that are subjected to great pressure so that they can break quite easily.

Thanks to her medical training, she could observe the process as it happened. Her account of how she was unable to ask for help is startling because she was even unable to remember phone numbers and, especially as she began to lose her sense of identity, her sense of ego, while at the same time, she felt a sublime sense of peace and joy difficult to explain in words. She also began to feel at one with everything around her rather than seeing things in her usual compartmentalized way. In her personal struggle to carry on she was not only unable to use language and ask for help but at the same time she felt such wonderful emotions that she wanted to remain just where she was. Finally, she was rescued; the surgery to remove the blood clot which was putting pressure on her brain did the trick, and eight years later she had completely recovered. She needed great strength to recover the concepts and knowledge that she had had beforehand and even to learn the skills and routines that she had previously been able to do effortlessly.

We can't be categorical about anything in science, but it seems as if much of the makeup of our identity, of our personality and of the patterns of our behaviour depends on the left brain hemisphere. This makes absolute sense if we consider the importance that language has in the construction of our identity and, up to a certain point, the way we interpret reality which affects the emotional experiences that we have. It is possibly in the left brain hemisphere where we can find the mental limits that we impose on ourselves and that are reflected in our filters when we come to observe reality. That said, as has been clearly shown in the case of Dr. Taylor, one can't make out shapes, numbers, letters and objects if we don't have at hand a left brain hemisphere working effectively.

Despite all this, if we want to learn new things and change some of the pre-established patterns so that they reflect our real circumstances, it seems evident that the right brain hemisphere is essential because it not only brings the experience of unity but also the complete absence of the sense of time.

If we only live on the plane of identity and personality, our life will be limited to playing safe in a comfortable environment and although we could use our learned skills and routines with ease we wouldn't be able to develop effectively.

We need both hemispheres but not one dominating over the other. Instead, we need both hemispheres to be working in close collaboration to take advantage of a sense of seeing things from different viewpoints or perspectives.

You have some very precious
capacities which enable
you to analyse and reason.
Nevertheless, don't forget that
you have other hidden talents
which are just as important.
Cultivate periods of silence and
reflection and you will begin
to see facets of reality that you
were not aware of beforehand.

4. THE TREASURE MAP

"Although we can't see any power in a glass of water,
  when it turns into vapour, it is able to move the pistons
  of very powerful machines."

T.T. LIANG

I f we want to understand how it is possible that we
have unknown strengths and resources hidden inside
ourselves, it is important that we explore the so-called
"treasure map". The maps of the ancient buccaneers were
by no means easy to read. These pirates had to be sure
that only those with the necessary tools could really make
sense of them. A great fortune awaited that person who
was aware, on the one hand, of the paths that had to be
avoided because of the many traps. And, on the other
hand, of the clues he would have to follow if he wished to
get to the prized booty.

Our mind is like a big map in which, in a more or
less opaque way, one finds clarity and light but also our

darkest shadows. That which propels us forward in life and that which acts as a ballast against achieving our goals and most-desired dreams. It is only from a perspective in which we can contemplate how the different parts of this map relate to each other, that we can design more effective action strategies.

Our mental map is in the form of a circle because a circle has neither a beginning nor an end. In this circle we can find two large areas. One of these, although present, is hidden. It is as if it was written with the invisible ink with which many secret documents were written and whose message only becomes visible by putting them near the light of a candle.

> *"We need to have the courage to enter into this other hidden world (our subconscious) [...] If we do this, we will discover two things: the origin of our involuntary behaviour and our unexplored potential."*

The other area that exists on our map is visible and there we will find all that we know we know and all that we know we don't know. In my case, I know that I know surgery. But, on the other hand, I know that I am not familiar with the Chinese language although I am aware that this culture and language exist. If I were sufficiently

interested I could begin to study some simple textbooks to get to know this language
and culture.

Our everyday consciousness has access to this area that contains what we know we know and what we know we are ignorant of. For this reason we are aware of it without much effort.

Much of our knowledge, ideas and experience are contained in this region available to our everyday awareness. Nevertheless, we need to go beyond what this area offers us if we are to resolve many of the problems we call complex as well as overcome the challenges that life throws in our direction when we do not have the previous experience required to sort them out. We need to have the courage to enter into this other hidden world. This other hidden world is our subconscious. If we do this, we will discover two things: the origin of our involuntary behaviour and our unexplored potential.

The first person in modern times who understood the immense role that the subconscious plays in our lives was Sigmund Freud. While observing Charcot in Paris, he began to work out his theory that much of our mental and emotional disorders were rooted in conflicts taking place at a subconscious level.

Human beings love to be in control of everything and we tend to rebel against the idea that much of our behaviour has a subconscious origin and, therefore, cannot be controlled in any way. We feel that this implies determinism and a lack of free will that is quite unacceptable. Despite this, nobody has said that we have no freedom, but rather if we don't understand how the subconscious works and how to form connections with it, it will continue to control many of the reactions to the events we face. Reactions which are not conducive to a balanced life.

Our conscious mind can be compared to the captain of a sailing boat, and our subconscious mind to the wind that fills the sails. Even if it is hard for him to admit it, the captain has to learn how the wind works (and to use it in his favour), or he won't get anywhere with his boat.

The part of our map that we can't see (because it is drawn with "invisible ink") also conceals a great treasure in the form of wisdom, energy, creativity, peace, joy and love. If we can get to this treasure, our lives will undergo a positive transformation in all senses of the word. That is why the map is so valuable.

We can also find in that hidden map, the great snares that will try to stop us from reaching the treasure trove. These traps remind us of those that Ulysses had to face in the Odyssey. The singing of the Sirens was so beautiful that the sailors, unable to resist such delightful music, steered their boats into the rocks, wrecked them and died. Ulysses, aware of the impending danger, ordered his men to put wax in their ears in order not to be seduced by the Sirens' singing whose only purpose was to bring them to perdition.

The snares which try to impede us from reaching the treasure, as we saw in the last chapter, are known as "mental filters" and their great power is based on their capacity to alter the perception of what we see, and they can lead us, in this way, to self-destruction without us even being aware of it.

> *"Our conscious mind can be compared to the captain of a sailing boat, and our subconscious mind to the wind that fills the sails. Even if it is hard for him to admit it, the captain has to learn how the wind works (and to use it in his favour), or he won't get anywhere with his boat."*

The most important thing to highlight now is that, while we are incapable of rising above those filters, while we can't get beyond them, we won't be able to get in touch with our real potential and with our real treasure trove.

The best way to alter the perception of what we see is by creating certain emotions. Isn't it true that when we get out of bed the wrong side we see people as being particularly unfriendly and it becomes more difficult to make an effort to do anything?

When a person is happy because something has turned out right, he or she tends to be more friendly and patient. They simply see things in a different light. For this reason, when we change our way of looking at things, those same things change.

These personal and collective filters have a great capacity to pass on (or not) data that we receive from our surroundings. Think of one of those small toy boxes we give to young children. Each side of the box, which is often red, has small openings of different shapes. Some of them are star-shaped, others the shape of the moon, others of fish and a whole lot of other ones too. The other part of the toy is formed of small pieces (generally yellow) and of diverse shapes like, for instance, a star, a moon or a fish. The child, so as to develop his motor cortex, has to find the side of the box which has a similar opening to the yellow piece he has in his other hand. When the piece he has in his hand is a fish and he tries to place it through the moon-shaped slit, however hard he tries, the boy will be unable to drop the piece inside the box.

Our mental filters function in a similar way. They have space to enable data from our surroundings to reach our consciousness, but if the filter is of one particular kind, some fragments of reality, even if they are as real as the child's fish, will not be perceived by our conscious selves.

I recall the case of a man I met who had been born and brought up far from what we term "civilization". When he got there and entered a cinema he couldn't understand what he had seen, as the only thing he had been able to perceive was a series of greys that were moving about in a crazy way. Even though all of us have visual areas in our brains that permit us to capture the images of a film, when a person does not have sufficient space on his mental filter for this to be possible, despite the senses perceiving the images, what that person will perceive will be profoundly distorted.

I know that this idea that our perception can be so limited may cause vertigo. Nevertheless, I'd like to invite you to see it from another perspective.

Are the opportunities that we see the only ones which exist?

Are we able to imagine the things that we could discover in ourselves, in others, and in the world if we could just get beyond what our filters allow us to see?

A FINAL WORD

Often what is most precious
is hidden from our eyes.
Approaching what we already
know with an open-mind can
help us to discover much more.

5. DRAWING THE MOST VALUABLE OF PICTURES

"A bad habit enters like a guest, joins the family, and finally, takes control."

THE TALMUD

To understand how we create our personality, we need to look into our past in order to realize the way certain mental processes took shape. If we keep on thinking that personality is something that, as adults, we have completely worked out, it will be more difficult to change those aspects of ourselves that we would really like to change. We have already seen the point at which our most profound beliefs affect our perception of reality.

I'd like us to be able to see our personality, our identity, not as a rigid, well-defined structure but rather as a process in constant transformation. If personality is a dynamic process, there must be certain forces which are moulding it; particular forces which give it stability and also some forces that can alter it. Understanding this play of forces is important if we wish to open ourselves up to a process of personal change.

To concentrate on the source of our personality, I'd like to ask you to try to recall one of those moments, perhaps in childhood, when you spent summer or another time of the year, beside the sea. Maybe on more than one occasion you went up to the water's edge to make some shape in the sand. Do you remember how desperate you felt when the wave, bigger than expected, washed away the object that you, possibly with a friend and with great effort, had built?

Something similar happens to us when we build our personality – in other words, when we create the description that we make of ourselves. Over time we build up something similar to the image in the sand, which in this case, would be a self-portrait that represents us. Each time that we say "I am like this" or "I'm not like this", we add new brush strokes to this painting, to this figure drawn in the sand. It is easy to come to the conclusion that, if I see myself in a given way, all the behaviour and every action that I carry out will be very much related to the way I see myself.

We define ourselves by getting information from our environment and, of course, from the people that we have around us, at home, at school, in the street. Every time that someone uses the verb "to be", he gives a piece of data that we tend to use when building our self-portrait. So, for example, if someone highly-respected says, "Why are you trying to do this if you aren't able to?", this comment can cause us to distort the picture we are creating for ourselves. People aren't aware of the importance that everything connected with the verb "to be" has, as it is from this verb that we build much of what makes up our personality. For this reason, those of us who have children, nephews and nieces or pupils have to be especially cautious and try our best not to make comments like, "You are untidy", "You are slow", "You are unable to do that" or "You are silly". It is generally more recommended to change the verb "to be" for other verbs: "It is untidy", "You act slowly", "You feel unable to do it" or "You have done something silly".

> *"People aren't aware of the importance that everything connected with the verb "to be" has, as it is from this verb that we build much of what makes up our personality."*

It seems obvious that we would soon come to realize that our self-portrait is merely a simple description that we have made of ourselves and that we are in fact much more than this. However, since this description of ourself began in the very early stages of our life, we don't realize just how much we stick to it and identify with it. Thus, this self-portrait is defined, and when life presents us with an opportunity in the form of a challenge, we consult this image of ourself. It's as if it is a "magic mirror" that given who we are reveals we can face such a challenge. If the mirror tells us we aren't able to, we will be crushed by feelings of hopelessness and being at a dead-end. It was for this very reason that the American philosopher, Emerson, stated that "The best present a friend can give us is to put in front of us a mirror that reflects a noble image of ourselves."

> **"** *Our self-portrait is merely a simple description that we have made of ourselves and that we are in fact much more than this.* **"**

Yet, when we come across a situation in life or simply another person who tries to change this image that we've created, we will resist just like the child who had his figure in the sand which was built with such effort altered by the sea wave. In some way, then, we've come to believe that that image, that this personality is ourself instead of understanding that it is simply a representation of ourself and that we are much more than this. It is surprising to see just how far we go to resist a change in this image.

Nevertheless, it is not difficult to understand if we take into account that our personality is something that we cling on to so as to know who we are. It is easy to understand our fear of this image changing because we feel sure that, if it does change, we'll be incapable of recognizing ourself.

I remember a student of mine studying on a Masters course in Human Resources who got really angry when I made the comment that I saw a precious diamond inside every human being. "Isn't there perhaps among us someone who is just a piece of dirty, black coal?"

It wasn't so much what he said but how he said it, the tension in his face and the hard tone of his voice. Since I consider that anyone who can recognize the diamond inside himself must be able to see some possibility in all other human beings, I felt perhaps that this student was just referring to himself.

There are people who are in a depressed state who don't wish to get better, even if it appears they do. At a subconscious level all their conscious desires to get over it are taken captive. In the depths of their minds, they are convinced that "I am like this and nothing can make this change".

How is it possible those human beings who believe themselves to be so intelligent, can fall into such a trap? Simply, as we have seen, because we create it without being aware that we are creating it.

In some parts of Asia, in order to capture certain kinds
of monkeys, they use a very curious trap which comes
to my mind and has some parallels with what we are
discussing. It is a wooden box tied to a tree. The box
has a circular hole that allows the outstretched hand
of the monkey to penetrate the inside of the box. Inside
the box there is some food which the monkey perceives
as appetizing and so all you need to do is wait. After
a while the monkey appears and starts to explore the
place, little by little placing his hand through the hole
and grabbing the food inside the box. With his fist
closed so he doesn't lose his prize, the monkey tries to
take his hand out of the box. But now that it is closed
and with the food in his hand, he cannot do this. That's
when the hunters come out of their hiding-place and
trap the monkey without any difficulty.

We are a bit like that monkey: we build an identity,
a personality, a description of ourselves and we cling on
to it. We don't want to let it go and when life tells us that
we need to free ourselves of this identity if we wish to
maintain our freedom, change or transform ourselves in
some way, we don't do it.

> *"There are people who are in a depressed state who don't wish to get better, even if it appears they do."*

There is a profound reason why we don't wish to let go of our identity and personality and, at least intellectually, it's easy to see why. When we have completely identified with this image and the image then disappears, we will feel we are dying, that we are disappearing. Therefore, it is not that we can't change but rather there is a huge resistance to change inside ourselves which we don't realize is there. It's a bit like a caterpillar that doesn't want to become a butterfly. I can imagine that the moment the caterpillar enters that dark space which is a cocoon, so that the protolithic enzymes liberates it from its identity as a caterpillar, only the confidence in mother nature with its superior intelligence can make it stay in the cocoon and begin its transformation into a chrysalis. When the cocoon opens, the creature that emerges is not a caterpillar but a butterfly. There hasn't just been a change but rather a complete transformation. Since its identity has been that of a caterpillar, flying has been a possibility (even if this has been unknown to the caterpillar). However, only its change into a butterfly has transformed this possibility into an extraordinary reality. The same thing happens to the acorn, which has inside itself the possibility of becoming an oak tree. However, until the acorn disappears, the oak cannot appear.

I want to ask you to make use of your imagination and put yourself in the skin of the caterpillar, an insect which moves very slowly, almost dragging itself along. Is it not true that a caterpillar is unable to jump from one branch of a tree to another without killing itself?

In the same way, a series of things which would be possible for us if we used all our potential, are not because they are not considered sensible things to do from the image we have of ourselves. In other words, we can only be what we give ourselves the power to be. That said, what is not sensible or at all reasonable from the perspective of a caterpillar (the possibility of flying) is perfectly reasonable and sensible from the perspective of the butterfly. In other words, every identity has a unique perspective from which he sees everything and he cannot reach another perspective until he is prepared to rise above his own identity and discover that we are not rigid beings with fixed and pre-determined roles in life, but rather creatures capable of expressing an astonishing creativity. So, what's needed is to discover our own magic.

A FINAL WORD

In life, when something is
really important for us and we
feel the fear of emptiness, we
have to have faith that when we
take a step forward, despite our
fear, our wings will unfold.

6. THE MOST BEAUTIFUL LEGACY

"Attention is the most valuable currency I have
to pay for my interior freedom."

GURDIEFF

The ruler of a great kingdom, who was very old, wanted to
make sure that, before abandoning this world, he imparted
an important lesson to his son. During the kingdom's most
difficult times, it was important to be firm and ensure that
peace and harmony would ultimately reign in the country.
But for some reason, the young Prince couldn't quite
understand what his father was saying.

"Yes, Father, I understand that for you serenity is very
important but I believe that cunning and power are more
important."

One day, when the King was riding his steed he had a
great idea.

"Perhaps what my son needs is not for me to repeat
the same thing over and over again but to demonstrate it to
him in some way." Carried away by this idea he ordered a
meeting of the most important members of his court to the
main hall of the palace.

"I want to organize a painting competition. The biggest and most important one ever to be held. The town criers must make it known throughout the world that there will be an extraordinary prize for the winner of the exhibition.

"Your Majesty," asked one of the nobles, "what is the theme of the exhibition?"

"The theme is serenity, balance. I will only give you one order," said the King. "Under no circumstances should you reject any work of art, however strange it appears or horror it should cause."

The nobles left, without fully understanding the surprising order that the King had given them.

From all the corners of the known world came marvellous paintings. Some of them showed calm seas, others clear skies in which a flock of birds glided across creating a sensation of calm, peace and serenity.

The nobles were enthused by such beautiful paintings. "Without a doubt, his Majesty is going to find it very difficult to choose the winning painting among such magnificent works of art."

Suddenly, before the shocked public, appeared a truly bizarre painting. Painted in dark tones and with little light, it reflected a rough sea in the middle of a storm in which huge waves were crashing violently against the dark cliff rocks. The sky was covered with enormous dark clouds.

The nobles looked at each other in disbelief and soon broke out in laughter and mockery. "Only an idiot would have entered a competition about serenity with a painting like this."

They were on the point of tossing it out of the room when one of the nobles interrupted them saying, "We have an order from the King which we cannot disobey. He told us that we couldn't reject any painting, however strange it might be. Although we haven't understood the point of this order, it was given by our King and we can't ignore it."

"All right," said another of the nobles, "but put this painting over there in that corner, where it can hardly be seen."

The day came for his Majesty the King to decide on the winning entry. On arriving at the exhibition hall, his face lit up. But as he made his way through the exhibition his face became more and more morose.

"Your Majesty, do none of these paintings satisfy you?" asked one of the nobles.

"Yes, yes they are very beautiful, there's no doubt about that, but there's something lacking in all of them."

The King had got to the end of the exhibition without finding what he so wished to find when, suddenly, he noticed a painting sticking out in a corner.

"What is that there which is hardly visible?"

"It's another painting, your Majesty."

"And why have you placed it so far apart from the others?"

"Your Majesty, it's a painting painted by a lunatic. We would have rejected it but following your orders about accepting all the paintings that were sent to us, we decided to place it in a corner so as not to affect the beauty of the rest."

The King, who had a natural curiosity, went up to the strange painting which seemed so difficult to appreciate. Then he did something which none of the other members of the court had done. He went nearer to it and looked at it in more detail. It was then that, all of a sudden, his face lit up and raising his voice, declared, "This is, without a doubt, the winning entry!"

The nobles glanced at each other, perplexed, thinking that the King had gone mad. One of them, shyly, asked him, "Your Majesty, we've never disputed your commands *but, what do you see in that painting to make it the winner?"*

"You hadn't looked properly, come closer."

When the nobles got up close, the King showed them something among the rocks. It was a small nest where there was a newly-born bird. The mother was feeding it, totally detached from the storm taking place around her.

The King explained to them that this was just what he wished to show to his son, the Prince.

"Serenity does not come from living in an ideal world as is reflected in the other paintings with their calm seas and clear skies. Serenity is the capacity to keep your attention on what is a priority for you, despite the difficult circumstances."

This tale shows us the point up to which we focus our attention can be a source of harmony or imbalance in our lives. If we decide to pay attention on that which depresses us or makes us feel uncomfortable, the "storms of our life", we will be overcome with stress and lose our sense of personal well-being. However, if we force our attention and decide to focus on what for us is of most importance, we will keep a clear and focussed mind when all those around us are feeling lost.

" The way in which we focus our attention can be a source of well-being or imbalance in our lives. "

It is for this important reason that we should train ourselves and exercise our capacity to maintain our focused attention. We should stay away from certain company, from those people who are like black holes, who take away our energy, efficiency and health. The kind of people who only seem to enjoy reminding us continually all that is wrong in the world, all that is impossible to achieve and all our own and others' defects. If we pay them too much attention we'll end up having their view of reality. Maybe they do this because they need to feel they can control others' lives. But if we are making use of our free will, this is not something we should choose.

Be the master of your attention. The price of freedom is to be permanently alert. Remember that wherever your attention may wander, your emotions and energy will also go. Where you place your attention will always make it more real for you.

7. JUMPING OFF THE CLIFF

"Those that think too much before stepping forward, spend their lives on one leg."

ANTHONY DE MELLO

On one occasion I was holding a conference to a group of people, explaining to them what was the zone of comfort – that area in which we've got used to living – when break-time arrived. One of the organizers of the session came up to me and mentioned that among the audience there was a lawyer who was an expert on counselling women who were the victims of physical abuse. I took the opportunity to go up to her, greet her and ask her a question.

"Could you please tell me something which I have never understood: Why do women return home when they know they are going to be physically abused?"

I had imagined she would answer by saying they did it for their children or because they didn't have enough money to live alone. But the answer I got was completely different.

First she looked at me with a surprised face and then, replied, "Mario, you have just explained it yourself. They go back home because the world beyond is very frightening and although the world they know will make them suffer, at least it is a world in which they know what to expect."

I am sure that this is only part of the answer and that on many other occasions there are further motives which lead these women to go back to their homes. Nonetheless, this experience was useful because it made me realize in some cases where holding on tightly to one familiar zone can make it impossible for us to enter into other areas of discovery and development.

Very often it is only when we reach this inspiring point of dissatisfaction, where we say "No more", "It's over", "I can't carry on like this", and we resolve to take a step forward, do we summon up the courage to pass from the familiar to the unknown. That said, on other occasions it is not necessary for us to have reached rock bottom, but quite simply something or someone inspires us to breakthrough our ostensible limits and take that metaphorical leap into the void. In that moment, "just when the caterpillar thought the world was ending, it in fact realized it was the beginning of its transformation into a butterfly".

I once read a lovely story. In fact, this story seemed to reflect what really happened in Ghana, Africa. A village in Ghana had been through a very difficult period and its people felt downtrodden and lost. One person told some of the villagers this story which was then passed from mouth to mouth and began to work up very potent feelings in their hearts. Little by little these human beings started to rebuild themselves (emotionally-

speaking), until they had completely recovered their joy and enthusiasm for life.

> *"Sometimes holding on to a familiar zone can stop us from entering other areas of discovery and development."*

Without a doubt there are stories that are capable of waking us up to other realities. Perhaps you will find this one will be like that for you.

There was a shepherd who lived in a shack near a wood and a short distance from a mountain where there was a farmyard full of hens and a herd of goats. That year there was a terrible drought which meant that most of the grass had dried up. So the shepherd decided to take his goats on to the mountain top, where there would probably be more humidity and therefore he could find some tender grass for his animals. So he did this, and after a long walk, he got close to the mountain peak. There the animals grazed for several hours until dusk and before the shepherd decided to return to the shack he lived in. As he was coming down the mountain, among the rocks with his herd, he saw something large which he immediately recognized as an eagle's nest. Getting close he noticed inside were two chicks, one of which was dead from the nest having fallen off the rock on

which it was perched. The other chick, despite making some small movements, seemed seriously injured.

The shepherd had no love of eagles because he saw them as his enemies. On some occasions they had attacked his goats and even taken some of his hens. Nevertheless, feeling pity, he bent down, took hold of the injured chick as carefully as he could and took it back to his shack. There he cured it as best he could and began to feed it with small pieces of meat, allowing Mother Nature to do the rest. The bird completely recovered and began to grow and grow until it became a magnificent example of an adult eagle.

From the moment the eagle became a full adult, things began to change. The shepherd, who initially had felt so proud of what he had done, started to feel increasingly disturbed by the presence of the bird. In some way, he couldn't stop emotive images entering his head and he remembered what birds like this one had done to his goats and hens.

One day, the shepherd came to a decision. He decided to abandon it in the woods, thinking that nature would help it to survive and take care of itself. The shepherd took it to the woods three times and each time the eagle kept hopping about on the ground.

Not knowing what to do to get rid of the bird, the shepherd thought hard and the most absurd idea came to his head: he would leave the eagle in the farmyard with his hens.

When the hens saw this bird that they feared so much enter the farmyard, they rushed into the hen coop as fast as they could to take refuge. They soon realized the strange behaviour of this creature which quietly kept to itself, and little by little they started to get used to it being there.

The years went by and the eagle got used to living like a hen. It ate the same food, it moved about like a hen and it even learned to emit the same sounds that the hens made.

Things stayed like this until one day a naturalist was passing through the area doing research on the eagles in that region and, on passing close to the shepherd's shack, contemplated the spectacle before his eyes, in disbelief: it was no more and no less than an eagle living in harmony with hens. He ran up to the door and loudly knocked on it. The shepherd, hearing the noise, leaped up and opened it.

"Who are you? What do you want?"

"I beg you to forgive me but I'm a naturalist and I am dedicated to the study of eagles and I've just seen something incredible, an eagle living among hens."

The shepherd understood perfectly the cause of the naturalist's shock and, after inviting him into his home, he told him the story of how he had found the bird, cured it and looked after it with his hens.

The naturalist listened attentively to the story until something shook him abruptly, something apparently trivial, as it was just a simple comment made by the shepherd.

"The animal has lived so long among the hens that I have no doubt at all that although it has the outward appearance of an eagle, inside itself it is nothing more than a hen."

"I am really sorry but I couldn't disagree more with you on this point," answered the naturalist. The shepherd felt a bit taken aback possibly because he felt nobody could know his animal as well as he did.

"If you are so convinced, why don't you go and show me by making it fly?"

The naturalist went out into the farmyard, took hold of the eagle and did the first thing that he could think about which was to throw it up into the air and shout, "Fly!" The animal fell like lead and hid itself inside the hen coop. The shepherd smiled in an ironic manner, although the naturalist had no desire to give in. So, he started to look around as if looking for a lost object until he saw a ladder a few metres away. He went up to it and he put it up against one of the walls of the shepherd's shack. He went into the barnyard again, got hold of the eagle and climbed the ladder with the bird until he reached the ceiling. From there, he threw the eagle into the air shouting, "Fly!" The poor bird fell like a ball of feathers against the ground and remained there a few seconds, bewildered. On recovering it pulled itself together and rapidly went in to the hen coop to hide.

The shepherd then said to him, "If you carry on like that you're going to kill my hen."

Despite all the evidence against it, and all the shepherd's criticisms, the naturalist was absolutely certain that the eagle's spirit would never die, and for this reason, he refused to accept defeat.

Suddenly, something on the horizon caught his attention.

"What's that we can see in the distance?"

"That's the mountain peak where I found the eagle when it fell out of the nest. Why?"

"Because I'm going to take it there, where it was born and maybe in that way it'll remember where its roots are and will realize it can fly."

"You're mad. You're a foolish man, unable to accept defeat. Don't you think you've had enough proof of how absurd your theory is, of that stupid idea that the spirit of an eagle never dies?"

The naturalist didn't even try to defend himself but simply set to work. He returned to the hen coop, grabbed the eagle and began to walk with his eyes set on that mountain peak. The shepherd, without really understanding why and seeing that it was getting dark, took a lantern and followed them. They climbed the mountain all night long without the naturalist having a clue as to how to wake the eagle's sleeping spirit.

When they got to the top of the mountain, to where the eagle had been born, it was daybreak. The naturalist then noticed something curious: the eagle had stopped looking at the sun. Without knowing quite why, the naturalist grabbed the bird by the scruff of its neck and forced it to look at the sun. When he did this, the eagle made some strange movements, opened his splendid wings and began to fly. That day the eagle remembered what it really was and recovered its true identity. It realized it wasn't a hen but an eagle.

An eagle isn't better than a hen but it can see 82 times better than a hen and so it can see its prey at a distance of more than two kilometres. Besides this, an eagle is capable of seeing landscapes that a hen couldn't even imagine in its wildest dreams. It is true that the life of hens is easier because they get fed, whilst the eagle has to hunt; nevertheless, the price the hen pays is perhaps too high because it is nothing less than the impossibility of exercising its freedom.

> **"***The training that truly offers results is not the kind which helps us to improve our false identity [...], but that which helps us to transcend that same identity to find out who we really are.***"**

Something similar to what happened to the eagle in the story happens to human beings. We have forgotten who we really are and consequently have taken on a new identity that leaves us empty inside, because it doesn't fit in with the way we live today (whatever we may have materially). In order to make up for this feeling of emptiness, we try to dress up this false identity so that it appears more exuberant and valuable. For this reason, we often dream of that person we would like to be and with that way of acting that we would like to act. Our personal and social lives are full of "shoulds", or "ought to's" and "you shouldn'ts". In this way, we have to be more cautious, and not be so naive. Also, we need to be more wary and not be so trusting of others. All these demands make perfect sense when you see yourself as having defects and lacking something, but they don't make sense when you understand what is beyond your apparent identity. It is a place full of intelligence, creativity and love. One that is naturally perfect, and therefore, complete.

So, the training that truly offers results is not the kind which helps us to improve our false identity so that we are as we and others wish us to be, but rather that which helps us to transcend that same identity to find out who we really are.

A FINAL WORD

You do not have to become anybody else than who you already are because, in essence, you are already perfect. That is, complete. The only thing that you perhaps need to discover is what really lies behind the words I AM.

8. THE DOORS OF PERCEPTION

"The body and the mind are not two independent entities, but rather form the two modes by which Man, with his rational and divided mind, perceives himself."

KARLFRIED VON DURKHEIIME

William Blake stated that, "If the doors of our perception were cleansed, reality would appear as it is, infinite. The world in a grain of sand, paradise in a flower, eternity in an hour and all that exists in the palm of my hand."

It is easy to understand that the reality which an ant perceives is not the same as that which we perceive although reality, with its obstacles, laws and demands, is the same for everybody. In this way, the law of gravity affects the ant in the same way as it affects us. The reality perceived is that area of total reality that we can pick up, thanks to our five senses and the body and brain processes that we possess. Pigeons perceive the magnetic fields of the Earth, but humans cannot pick them up without the help of specialist equipment. Dogs perceive ultra-sounds whilst we cannot.

The data that is captured by our senses so that we can perceive it (that's to say, realize it exists) has a long way to go. Nonetheless, we get the impression that everything happens instantaneously.

> **"**There are states of mind which give us great competitive advantages and others that are very dysfunctional [...] and besides, have the capacity to harm the relationships we have with others.**"**

Emotions and states of mind are among the factors that most alter our perception. The first thing we need to do is to see the difference between what an emotion is and what a state of mind is. One of the basic differences lies in the notion of time. An emotion is a physical phenomenon which brings about a series of physiological changes that affect our hormones, our muscles and our viscera. These changes are limited in time to minutes or possibly several hours. For example, when an internal event (an anxious thought) or an external one (an insult) has affected us, the emotional reaction that has been triggered will little by little fade away until we get back to the physical state we were in prior to this thought or insult.

A state of mind is something much more prolonged in time as it can last days, months or years. In some ways it is as if we are frozen in a given emotion up to the point where we can even identify with it. It is as if it has formed part of our personal reality. Therefore, we have emotions and we live in states of mind.

There are states of mind which give us great competitive advantages and others that are very dysfunctional and cause us enormous suffering, a loss of efficiency and, besides, have the capacity to harm the relationships we have with others.

The true importance of a state of mind is not so much in how it makes us feel, although this is without a doubt important. The true importance of a state of mind is that, by itself, it has the capacity to alter profoundly the way in which our brain and body behaves. There are states of mind which generate health and vitality. They can also help to spread intelligence and creativity. These are states of mind which favour the connection between people, collaboration and teamworking. There are states of mind which do just the opposite. States of mind affect people individually and collectively in families, cities and countries. Let's remember, for example, the state of mind in Germany which existed there after the First World War, when, besides the enormous economic debt to the victorious countries, there were six million unemployed.

To be able to hold our attention on what is relevant and with the aim of seeing things with a certain perspective, we need specific parts of the brain to be especially active. This implies, on the part of the neurons which make up these areas, the need for them to receive an extra dose of energy in the form of glucose and oxygen. So then, the states of mind that characterize hopefulness, confidence and enthusiasm are associated with an increase in the blood levels in the left pre-frontal zone of the brain, whilst the states of mind characterized by anxiety, desperation and frustration show a lowering of the blood flow at that level. The left pre-frontal cortex is a key player in maintaining the personal balance and emotional homeostasis. Thanks to this we can see things with more perspective and clarity.

Reality is what it is. Nevertheless, depending on our capacity to keep a balance, we can find ourselves living in one kind of reality or another without realizing that we can choose.

Let's imagine, for example, a house with different rooms in which various events are taking place. In one of them there are three people fighting. In another of the rooms there are six people designing a project that will make them very rich. In a third room there's a marvellous library and there's a door that leads out into a lovely garden.

Reality is represented by the whole house in which all this is happening simultaneously. What's happening is that those in a particular room do not know that there are other rooms in which they can choose to be. Our states of mind "place us" , without us being aware of it, into one or other of the "rooms", unaware of the parallel universes and spaces that reality actually offers us. The person who is often moody will often find himself in the room where there are people fighting. The person who feels confident and hopeful will find himself talking to people and meeting others that generate prosperity and abundance. The person who is trying to find himself will be studying in the library and looking for inspiration in different authors. There will come a time when this person will realize there is a door that was always there that doesn't lead him to a different place but rather to himself, to his true essence, his real nature.

> *"If we do not substitute our involuntary reactions for voluntary ones, we will not be able to affirm that we are truly free in our deepest selves."*

I know that it is very difficult not to feel hurt when someone verbally attacks you and it is also very hard to remain joyful and hopeful in the midst of adversity. However, it is absolutely critical to be able to recover the space that exists between what happens to you and your response to it.

If we do not substitute our involuntary reactions for voluntary ones, we will not be able to affirm that we are truly free in our deepest selves. In later chapters we'll look at strategies to open up this area of freedom and transcend those involuntary reactions that only bring suffering and loss to our lives and the lives of those around us.

When you see a person, do not just take note of the human being that stands before you. Fix your attention on the state of mind that person has at that moment. It will be very difficult for you to connect with that person if you both have not got into a suitable state of mind.

9. QUESTIONS THAT HEAL AND QUESTIONS THAT CAUSE SICKNESS

"The body follows the mind like the shadow follows the substance."

T.T. LIANG

Our false identity, the one that wants us to take it as who we really are, needs to be in charge of our emotions because it is in this way that it controls our perception of things. So, for example, if we have identified ourselves as a depressed person, it is necessary for us to generate a perception that cancels out all beauty and joy in our life. All that is light and inspiring has to be replaced with horrible, obscure thoughts. For this reason the depressed individual cannot see any hope because his perception ensures everything is painted black.

It is not easy for this person who suffers so much and spreads their suffering to so many others to accept the possibility that it could be himself (without being aware of it) as the one who is generating these dysfunctional emotions. Therefore we need to move on two planes: one which perceives what we appear to be and the other what we really are. The plane of what we are aware of and the plane of what we are unaware of.

Now it might be interesting to know just how our imposter identity manages to produce these states of mind that alter our vision of things.

Our false identity takes command of three things. The first of these is the attention of which we have already spoken. Our imposter identity makes us pay attention in whatever it wishes us to fix our attention on and nothing else. If I, for example, enter a bedroom and only see what I dislike, there won't be any room in my mind for those things I do like.

We are going to carry out a little exercise to try to understand this better. I would like to ask you to turn your head, to the left and right, and search for something yellow for 30 seconds.

I assume that when I asked you to do this exercise you will have tried to find all the yellow objects. Now, I'd like to ask you about those objects which are purple. If you haven't seen any, turn your head again and take a look please. Our attention is selective and tends only to see what we actively look for.

I'll give you another example. If you are a woman and have been pregnant at some moment, you will have noticed just how many pregnant women you begin to see on the street.

If you are thinking of buying a red or a black car, you will notice how you begin to see many cars of these colours. This astonishing phenomena is all down to the fact that in the brain there's a structure called "Ascending Reticular Activating System" (RAS) whose mission is to direct the attention towards that which is most relevant for us. We have a selective attention and so "what the heart wishes to feel, the mind will show".

One of the quickest and most powerful ways of getting our attention fixed on a certain place is by means of asking questions. Every question is an invitation to look in a particular direction. Perhaps, for this reason, Einstein told us that the key is not finding the answer to old questions but in making new questions, ones which have never been formulated before. When Science questions something, this simple question has the capacity to open up a whole new line of research. So, the young Einstein, riding his bike on one occasion, made himself a question: "What would happen if I went at the speed of light and lit my headlight? Could you see it?" He reflected on this question for ten years. The result was the formulation of the Theory of Relativity.

By applying this more to our daily lives we will realize the power the questions we make can have over us. For example, if when I make a mistake, I ask myself, "Why do I keep doing such stupid things?", my ascending reticular activating system will look for the causes of it and will respond with answers such as, "I'm a bit thick", "I don't know enough" or "It's because I'm always alone". I would like to ask you to ask yourself if, when you have responded like this, you have created new opportunities to improve things or if you have become even more depressed?

> **"*Einstein told us that the key is not finding the answer to old questions but in making new questions, ones which have never been formulated before.*"**

Being in control of our focus of attention, as we've seen so many times, is so important that we can't allow ourselves the luxury of not training it. In order to train this skill we have at least two very useful and practical strategies.

The first of these strategies consists of putting all our attention on what we are doing in every moment. It would be like accepting that where we are and what we are doing in that precise moment is the most important thing of all. That's to say, we wouldn't wish to be anywhere else nor would we wish to be doing anything different. When we embrace the present moment, when we fully accept it, when we act as if we've chosen it, we transcend our mental limits and start to discover things which had previously been hidden from view.

In the world of medicine we know that the power of questions when trying to overcome a disease is so great that we have to be very aware of it when helping the patient who has been diagnosed with a serious health problem. When a person is told that he has a serious illness, rest assured he won't want to be there, never mind listening to what he is being told. However, when he accepts the present moment and comes to terms with the reality (in other words, when he accepts the situation), he will be able to free himself of fear, anxiety, rage, frustration and desperation.

I, due to my profession as both a doctor and surgeon, have had to tell another human being many times that he is suffering from a serious disease. Therefore I can understand the shock and devastation that those words produce, even when said with great care and love. Nevertheless, I believe that to get trapped in a state of mind full of anxiety and desperation is the worst possible position that we can adopt in order to overcome the disease.

The people who remain trapped for weeks and months with the constant question of "Why me?", without realizing it, generate enormous stress within themselves along with an increase in cortisol in their blood stream. Cortisol is a hormone which segregates the suprarenal glands in a physiological way. These glands are located above the kidneys. When the levels of cortisol in the blood are normal and follow the circadian rhythms, there is no problem. However, when we are pressurized by states of mind such as rage, fear or desperation, the levels of cortisol increase and this hinders the well-functioning of the immune system, which is what protects us from bacteria, viruses and tumours.

The question "Why me?", to start with, has no answer. Besides, it doesn't help us in any way. We know, however, that the body responds in a completely different way if we make other questions such as, "What can I do to get over this?" or "What can be positive about what's happening to me?" Not only do the states of mind that facilitate this type of question prevent cortisol levels increasing, but moreover, if we insist on the question, our ascending reticular activating system will respond in some way. Perhaps it will show us a way to fight the disease and get better. But without the right questions, this road could remain hidden from our sight.

Negative states of mind bring about harm in the digestive system as well as in the cardiovascular one. Furthermore, they can result in impotence and infertility.

I would now like to speak about a subject related to states of mind and health which is at the cutting edge and so surprising that it is difficult to believe. How would you feel if it was demonstrated to you that states of mind also affect our genes?

Dr. Elisabeth Blackburn is one of the world's leading experts in the study of telomeres and has won the Nobel Prize for Medicine and Physiology for her scientific studies. We know that we have structures which are known as "chromosomes" and that they have the form of an "X". Inside the chromosome is the DNA; the functioning units of the DNA are called "genes". We've all heard of the great importance that genes have in our life as they determine the colour of our eyes as well as the possibility that we will suffer certain diseases or not. Anyway, each extreme of this X that is the chromosome is wrapped up in a kind of hood that is known as "telomere". The function of the telomere is to prevent the chromosome from deflecting, because if this occurs the life of the chromosome will be reduced and, therefore, the person will get older quicker.

"The true encounter of human beings is not only one of the best anti-depressives that exist, but it also prolongs life."

As the telomere wears out in time, there's an enzyme inside the nucleus of the cell where the chromosomes are, known as "telomerase". Enzymes are substances which greatly accelerate the speed at which certain chemical reactions take place in the cell. The function of the telomerase is to repair the telomeres as they get worn down. What is truly interesting is the observation that there are lower levels of telomerase in those people who are trapped in dysfunctional states of mind. In this way, then, some of our imposter identities are actively generating states of mind that gravely deplete our health, favouring ageing and susceptibility to illness.

People that have a network of other people around them who love them and take care of them do not experience this reduction in telomerase levels. Neither do people who feel supported in moments of great difficulty.

The true encounter of human beings is not only one of the best anti-depressives that exist, but it also prolongs life. Maybe, taking into account this research, the role of communication should reassert itself in our lives and is something that should never have been lost in the first place.

A FINAL WORD

Very often the most relevant
thing is not to impart
knowledge or give explanations
but formulate questions which
allow us to explore things
which we had never even
considered before.

10. WORDS CREATE REALITIES

"Behind depression is aggression against oneself."
SIGMUND FREUD

There's a second mechanism by which the imposter identity can alter our state of mind and that is the use of language. Language does not only describe but creates our reality. Words automatically and rapidly open "emotional boxes". The type of emotional box they open depends on the experiences that we associate with those words.

The fact that language has access to this personal emotional world, both intimate and unique to each individual, is quite logical if we understand that we all use words to interpret what is happening to us. It is through our interpretations and the value we attach to the events that affect us, that we establish our certainties and convictions. These, little by little, make up our identity, our personality. It is these convictions installed in our subconscious which become our point of reference when it comes to determining what significance we are going to attach to particular events.

On one occasion I was invited to participate in a television programme about leadership. Among the guests was the president of an organization, a well-known social psychologist and a woman whose profession I won't reveal for the time being.

Before entering the studio, we were invited for a drink that served as a way for us to present ourselves to each other. I got the sensation that, listening to the profile of the woman guest, it was important that we came to some kind of conclusion as to what each of us understood by the term "leader". I put my point across clearly but the presenter replied that each of us would do this during the programme.

The programme began and the presenter, after presenting each one of us, began asking the president of the company what a leader meant to him. The man explained what for him a corporate leader was. Up until this point all went well and the programme ran naturally and smoothly.

After the first guest had spoken, it was my turn and the presenter asked me the same question. I made the point that for me a leader was a person capable of getting the best from himself and of inspiring others through his example.

While I was speaking, I also noticed how the woman was looking at me and how she was frowning more and more and more and her body was getting tense. Suddenly, she stood up and, in a provocative tone and making a great fuss, began to address me, as if, on the one hand I had offended her and on the other, she'd completely forgotten we were in a TV studio.

"That's not a leader. A leader is someone who brainwashes you, manipulates you and makes a slave of you. That is a leader and not what you are saying."

I remember how the presenter was almost speechless, taken completely by surprise by such an extreme reaction.

I would like to ask the reader, "What do you think was that woman's job?"

If we recall that words have the capacity to open experience boxes, the box which that woman must have opened when I spoke of what I understood by leader must have brought back very painful memories.

Now I feel I can reveal her profession: she was the leading expert in sects in that country. We all know the devastating effects that certain "leaders" of sects have had on their followers.

Language is so powerful that it is only necessary for a person to change, for example, the phrase "this is something terrible" for "this is inconvenient" for him to note, albeit subtly, a change in his emotional world. Let's remember that, on the surface, words are simple signs that correspond to certain sounds, but in reality they are direct connections to personal, intimate and unique emotional worlds.

This capacity which by itself can affect our emotions and states of mind is known as "transformational language". On this subject, some fascinating research has been carried out to measure the impact that words have on our individual physiologies and on our bodies.

A group of volunteers were brought together in a hospital in the United States and they were asked to observe a series of words with negative connotations projected onto a wall for a few minutes. For example, among the words were "impossible", "complex", "unattainable", "dangerous", "disagreeable" and "frightening". Then a sample of saliva from each volunteer was taken to measure hormones using a technique called radioimmunoassay

The second part of the experiment consisted of the volunteers looking at words projected on the screen which had a much more positive connotation. Among the words that appeared were "possible", "accessible", "achievable", "capable" and "valuable". Afterwards, saliva samples for radioimmunoassay were taken again.

The results were quite curious as in the first task, the group showed a considerable rise in cortisol, whilst in the second one, facing the vision of the more positive words, the same group of volunteers showed a fall in the cortisol figures.

We already know how cortisol is associated with very profound changes in the functioning of the body and brain. We cannot continue to ignore the fact that if we keep on using negative words, we not only are doing nothing to resolve the problems that these same words describe but, moreover, we are making it much more difficult. I am not speaking of getting rid of these negative words from our vocabulary but rather of modulating their use. To take an example, the effect of saying to somebody that something is impossible is not the same as saying it is improbable.

All experience is the coming together of an event, an emotion and an interpretation of it. We alter our experiential memories when we change the way we interpret what is happening to us.

> " Remember that words have an enormous power when it comes to affecting the type of experience that we create. "

Years ago, psychologists and psychiatrists in the United States gave a very serious warning to families of women who had been raped. This is because they discovered that such a traumatic event with such an emotional charge could leave a much worse mark on these women if the families around them went to the hospital or police station to visit them and made accidental blunders. The families, besides sympathizing with the rape victim, would add comments like, "I did tell you not to go to such dark places", "We did tell you that we didn't like that boy at all", or "The trouble is you're too trusting. We said you can't trust anybody so many times to you".

Now that we know how the memory is recalled and the importance of interpretation, we can understand that along with the event itself, the emotions and value judgements that these women had made, facilitated by these comments, created in the victim new thoughts such as, "Yes, I am really stupid" , "I'm just so naive" or "I don't do anything right". These judgements can generate very intense feelings of guilt and shame that make these individuals feel even smaller and more limited.

For this reason, it was suggested to these families to silence their desire to indoctrinate and change the message in such a way that those women, who'd been through such a gruelling experience, would feel supported rather than self-pitying. It was suggested they use comments such as, "How brave you've been, despite what you've been through, to ask for help" or "You've shown such strength and you're showing such fortitude that you're bound to get over this".

We need to remind ourselves of the great power that words have in affecting the type of experience that we create. These kinds of value judgement have the capacity to alter the memory even though they have not changed the actual event, the thing itself.

There is a very thought-provoking tale that comes from Japan and it reminds us of the extraordinary power of words and their capacity to alter our emotions.

Once upon a time there was a samurai who was very dexterous with the sword and at the same time, haughty and arrogant. In some way, he only felt important when he killed an adversary in combat and, for this reason, he was always looking for occasions to challenge someone for the most trivial reason. It was in this way that the samurai held onto his idea, his concept of himself, his iron-clad identity.

On one occasion, this man arrived at a village and saw that a crowd of people were all going towards a particular place. The samurai halted one of them and asked him, "Where are you all going in such a hurry?" "Noble warrior," answered the man, who probably feared for his life, "we're going to listen to Master Wei."

"Who is this man Wei?"

"How is it possible that you don't know him if Master Wei is known throughout the region?"

The samurai was made to feel stupid by this villager and he noticed the respect that the man felt towards this so-called Master Wei and that he didn't feel for a samurai like himself. He then decided that this day his fame would outdo Wei's and so he followed the crowd until they arrived at a huge ranch where Master Wei was imparting his knowledge.

Master Wei was a short, elderly man for whom the samurai immediately felt great contempt and barely-disguised wrath.

Wei began to speak:

"There are many powerful weapons used by man in this life, but for me, the most powerful of all is the word."

When the samurai heard that he just couldn't contain himself and he exclaimed in midst of the multitude: "Only a stupid old man like you can make such a comment."

He then took out his sword and wielding it about in the air, continued, "Yes, this is a powerful weapon and not your stupid words."

Then Wei, looking him in the eyes, answered, "It makes sense that someone like you would have made such a comment; it's easy to see you are nothing more than a bastard, an ignorant brute, a being without any intelligence and a son of a bitch."

When the samurai heard these words, his face reddened and with his body tensed and his mind outraged he moved towards the place where Wei was.

"Old man, take leave of your life because today it ends." Then, all of a sudden, Wei began to apologize.

"Forgive me, great man. I am just an old, tired man. Someone who, due to his age, can have the most serious slips of the tongue. Will you be able to forgive this fool, who in his madness has injured you so, with your noble warrior heart?"

The samurai stopped short and answered, "Naturally, noble Master Wei. I accept your excuses."

In that moment Wei looked him straight in the eyes and told him, "My friend, tell me now: are words powerful or not?"

The tale says that in that one moment the samurai understood how what for him were simple words had had the capacity to alter him in more ways than many of his former rivals. He also understood how the words had brought him back to serenity and a balanced state of mind which he hadn't had for a long time. In that moment something inside him began to transform.

Therefore let's be cautious with the type of words we use and with the type of value judgements that we make so that it's not the events, but our own personal judgements which rob us of our personal power and generate unnecessary suffering.

A FINAL WORD

Words are not blown away
by the wind but rather create
realities. Search for words
that help and do not nullify.
Perhaps you'll be surprised by
what begins to happen.

11. HOPE FOR VICTORY AND YOU'LL BE VICTORIOUS

"We are chained to ways of walking, ways of thinking and ways of perceiving and feeling. We are slaves to our automatic behaviour."

F.M. ALEXANDER

The third element to which our identity has to have access is our body, our physiology. Given that neither emotions nor states of mind could exist without a body, direct access to our body quickly gives rise to an emotional change. One can reach the emotions through the body in various ways.

The first of these is body posture, the level of muscular stress and the way we move. We are so used to thinking that everything is controlled from the brain, and by often thinking this, we don't want to believe that a simple change in body posture or in the way we move can have such great impact on the way we feel, perceive and reason.

If you do physical exercise you may have had the following experience: you've had a hard day dealing with difficult people, with never-ending meetings, and you feel without energy, physically and mentally exhausted. You've spent time reflecting over it, thinking it over and over in your head, and you don't notice any less stress or more clarity, and of course, your exhausted state remains unchanged. Then you decide to put on some trainers and loose clothing and you go for a jog. At first, the thoughts bombard you, but a time comes when they begin to stop and you are much more involved in what you are doing; that is, jogging. It wouldn't be a surprise if when you stop jogging you feel you have much more energy and are more clear-headed. Also that you feel more relaxed and more able to see the events from a different perspective.

It remains surprising how the body is capable of resolving what the head, however hard it tried, could not. In order that you get an idea of how important it is to move your body, to have a little walk, to do exercise, I'd like to state that it is not only associated with a reduction in premature deaths but also produces an increase in generating neurons in areas of the brain necessary to learn new things. Moreover, this area known as the "hippocampus" is very important in regulating amygdala nuclei found in the brain, just in front of the hippocampus and which provokes reactions of panic and rage. Haven't you noticed that when you change your sedentary life for one of greater mobility, you feel less affected by events which could be described as negative? This is due to the fact that the hippocampus modulates the amygdala so that they do not start up with the slightest stimulus.

The importance of posture, in aspects which on the surface have no bearing (like managing one's emotions), are practised and known about in Yoga and other disciplines. In the West it was Matthias Alexander who probably most demonstrated to us everything related to this basic aspect of our physiology.

Frederick Matthias Alexander was born in 1869 in Tasmania (Australia). He was a Shakespearean actor. There came a time when Alexander began to have a very serious problem with his voice. In the middle of a theatrical performance, he remained speechless. I think we can imagine what it meant for someone whose vocation and profession was acting, to lose his voice.

Even though Alexander consulted several medical specialists, none of them could find either the cause of his condition, much less the solution or even a partial solution. Faced with this situation, this exceptional man, instead of giving up or getting desperate, began to do research to find an answer to the question, "What is happening to me?"

Making use of mirrors, the first thing he realized was that his sensory reference systems weren't giving him correct information. When he had the sensation that his head was turned in a certain way, on passing in front of a mirror he realized his head was protruding more forward or more backward than he thought.

His second great discovery was that the body has its own systems of righting itself but that we block them out with a series of mental patterns and involuntary actions that are reflected in the way that we use our body. For Alexander, if we avoid dysfunctional behaviour, by simply realizing it and correcting it, only that which is functional will appear. Therefore, for him, the key was first of all to be aware and then to inhibit the wrong reaction and, finally, to drive it in the right direction.

All important personal change requires similar steps. First, to step from the subconscious incompetence to conscious incompetence. This implies a rise in the level of awareness. In other words, the capacity for us to realize something that we hadn't realized before.

The second step is from the conscious incompetence to the conscious competence. What we need to do at this point is to use our strength of will and our determination to do what we have decided to do even if it's difficult. This is a very hard phase because we are constantly fighting so that the old involuntary behaviour does not over-pressure us.

The third and last step is from conscious competence to subconscious competence. That means, we have created a much healthier and beneficial habit.

Not paying attention to the automatic reactions will lead us, little by little, to the manifestation of a more natural answer. In some way, the correct behaviour cannot occur until we have given up the wrong behaviour.

"Many habits close doors and what we have to do is open them by paying more attention to what we do.'

Matthias Alexander was aware that the way we use ourselves affects our states of mind and that by sitting down in the right way, moving in a suitable way and speaking by holding the head up in a balanced way has repercussions not only in how you feel but also in your level of clear-thinking and even in the power of your voice.

Alexander attached more importance to the direction you went in than the objective itself. Aware of just how deeply-rooted were many of our habits, it was essential that we were clear where we wished to go, without worrying about the cost. The right way appears to spread itself out and our mission is simply not to get in the way. Only confidence and determination that the change will occur sooner or later, is what makes people carry on and not give up.

Many habits close doors and what we have to do is open them by paying more attention to what we do. This means paying attention without passing judgement as what we are after is simply to increase our capacity of observation.

Alexander invited us to give much more freedom to our necks, to liberate part of their great stiffness. He also encouraged us to allow our bodies to enlarge themselves and to expand, abandoning those restrictive and contracted body postures.

Matthias Alexander not only recovered and made his voice more powerful as an actor but he also helped many people in the world to recover body functions which had been lost.

Methodologies like Yoga, Tai chi Chuang or Qi Gong are so potent and effective because they also help us to find harmony and balance in our minds through body movement. All of them, for thousands of years, reveal something fascinating: the body has a wisdom that the mind cannot understand.

The body is the subconscious, and for this reason, when you look after your body, you are taking care of your mind; and when you take care of your mind, you also take care of your body.

12. THE FUEL OF LIFE

"Nobody really sees a flower;
it's so small and most of us really don't have time
and to see takes time."

GEORGIA O'KEEFE

W e cannot speak of the impact that body posture
or movement has on our states of mind without
also speaking of something that is very relevant to
our emotional world. I am speaking about breathing,
something that seems so mundane to us that we hardly pay
attention to it.

The moment we breathe when we are born marks our
entrance into this world. The moment we stop breathing
marks our exit from it and our trip to another dimension.

If we are attentive to the changes in our breathing
we will realize immediately that they inform us that a
mental and emotional change is taking place. Depression
has its own way of constraining breathing, limiting the
movement of the diaphragm. Anxiety generates a rapid

and superficial breathing that increases the levels of lactic acid in the blood which, in turn, generates a greater level of anxiety.

Breathing exercises are very important for helping us free ourselves of those emotional shields that we have developed throughout our lives. Musicians and actors, before coming on stage, make sure they have a few minutes to take a number of deep breaths to calm themselves down.

Returning to a pattern of calm, abdominal breathing has a powerful calming effect and, for this reason, is so useful in complicated situations in the operating theatre, or when faced with a fight in the street, or when we are at home and something happens which unbalances us.

"Breathing exercises are very important for helping us free ourselves of those emotional shields that we have developed throughout our lives."

Breathing, besides its physiological impact, is of great use in cultivating that faculty that we have spoken of so much – our capacity for concentrating and paying attention. If you just simply close your eyes for a few minutes and concentrate on the movements we make when breathing, even counting them, you will notice how calm, peaceful and serene you feel for those few moments.

The simple fact of stopping the worried thoughts that so often invade our consciousness has a clear and healthy effect as it reduces our internal stress and produces bodily relaxation.

If you have problems getting to sleep, I suggest that you do the following exercise and you'll see how, when you manage to relax your body, you'll end up relaxing your mind and you'll finally get to sleep.

The first step is to start paying attention to the gentle movements of your breathing. After that, imagine that the air is moving from your navel to the part of the vertebral column which is at the same height as the navel. In other words, you are going to imagine that the air enters your navel and reaches the lower part of your back and then, when you breathe out, it goes in the opposite direction. After counting 15 times breathing in and out, do the same but to the height of the heart. So imagine the air in the top part of the chest goes backwards until it reaches the part of the vertebral column located at the same height. It is as if there is a tunnel connecting the front of the body with the back. After that, while breathing out, invert the movement and the air enters from behind and goes out on the front at the height of your heart. You should also count and breathe about 15 times in and out.

The last breathing exercise is done at the height of the neck. The air enters at the height of the larynx and goes out of the back of the neck. On breathing out the air, it enters through the back of the neck and goes out through the front part of the larynx. Count 15 times breathing in and out.

Don't get anxious thinking if you are going to fall asleep or not because, even if you don't fall asleep (which is highly unlikely), this exercise is by itself very beneficial for your health.

Recovering sleep, when you've lost it, is essential. This society in which we live is experiencing a great sleep deprivation syndrome and this can have serious effects on our levels of efficiency and health. Adults need to sleep an average of between seven and eight hours a day. Little children need more. Getting used to sleeping less does not mean that your body (sooner or later) won't suffer the consequences. Sleep is very important for the memory as it affects how everyday experiences are integrated and stored along with all the other files in our brains.

During sleep, our immune system which protects us from bacteria, viruses and tumours is especially active, which means it patrols and destroys the bad agents that have entered our body.

When we regularly do not sleep a sufficient number of hours, the body alarm system is immediately activated and so our levels of energy, vitality and clear-thinking are weakened. It is absurd to think that "we'll sleep enough when we die". That kind of comment reveals a profound ignorance of the way in which our organism functions. While we look at our hours of sleep as a waste of time and not as an investment, we will never give priority to this aspect of our lives. The less you sleep, the less you can do and so you have to work more hours, which means the hours you have for sleep are fewer. In the end we get trapped in a vicious circle out of which it is difficult to escape.

> " *During sleep, our immune system [...] is especially active, which means it patrols and destroys those bad agents that have entered our body.* "

Finally, closing our eyes for between ten and 20 minutes after eating has a beneficial effect which has been demonstrated in multiple studies. It improves our state of mind, capacity to concentrate, efficiency and health.

Watching horror films at night and listening to bad news reports before going to bed (according to some studies) have a negative impact on the sleep process.

To sum up, I'd like to highlight something that is very important in the case of children. The growing hormone, called "GH", performs at its peak at midnight. Children that are still growing and regularly stay up watching the television can have their growth reduced due to less of this hormone being released.

To recover the value of sleep in our lives is something that we all have to fight for. Our society, in this regard, is going along a different road from what is actually appropriate for our health.

When you feel tense or confused, remember that the first thing you have to do to feel calm and relaxed is get in control of your breathing. It is the quickest, most efficient and direct step by which to return to a balanced state.

13. THE CELLULAR BRAIN

"Love is not love
Which alters when it alteration finds"

JAMES HILLMAN

The researchers Watson and Crick discovered DNA and the way that its sequence determines the creation of those proteins that end up becoming who we are. Since then, there has been great interest in new discoveries in respect to the human genome. It seemed so logical to think that if the DNA was found in the inside of the cell nucleus, this would give the said nucleus the category of "cellular brain". However, allow me to ask you this question: "Does the brain make decisions or just carry them out?" Although the answer is not as simple as it may seem, we can basically affirm that the answer is that the brain is fundamentally what takes decisions which the other organs have to carry out. Therefore, if this were the case, the "cellular brain" would not be found in the cell nucleus despite having the DNA inside it. The DNA carries out a series of orders so that some of the genes that are functional units of DNA are activated or not. Not even monozygotic twins that share exactly the same DNA sequence have the same personality or suffer the same diseases. There is something else which has somehow escaped our attention for so long.

Surrounding the cell cytoplasm which is the place where we find the "energy centre", consisting of the cell named "mitochondrial" as well as the granulated endoplasmic reticula (which are where the proteins are produced), we find the so-called "cellular membrane". So that we are aware of the importance of the membrane for cell life, it will be suffice to say that we can get rid of the cell nucleus without killing the cell itself. That said, it couldn't synthesize new proteins nor could it reproduce itself into two daughter cells but it won't die for many days. If, on the other hand, we eliminate the cell membrane, it will die instantaneously.

Today it is becoming much clearer that the real cell "brain" is not in the nucleus but rather in the membrane. It is the membrane which is in contact with all the chemical substances that flow through the blood. These include "emotional molecules" to elements which have entered our body from the environment. It is the cell membrane, with its multiple receptors or entrance doors, which becomes extremely sensitive to the chemical environment in which it lives. There are molecules which, either acting indirectly through the membrane or having direct influence on the nucleus, result in certain genes stepping into action or not. This data is of enormous relevance as we have already seen, because it points very clearly towards the possibility that people, depending on our habitual state of mind, can favour the expression of one kind of gene and not others. Every day it is becoming clearer that, even though medicine can help us in many ways to combat illness, we also have a clear influence in keeping that illness at bay. We can also have a positive effect when attacking this illness when we are suffering it. This is why those people who are positive thinking often improve their chances of getting better.

"When a person has got used to living trapped with a determined personality, he has also been confined to living in a kind of box, an authentic prison [...]"

We now need to leap to concepts of another nature in order to understand something, which otherwise would be incomprehensible to us. When a person has got used to living trapped with a determined personality, he has also been confined to living in a kind of box, an authentic prison, without realizing it. This area, which is so familiar to us and we call the "comfort zone", is profoundly limiting, because it deprives us of what we have spoken about so much which is to be free inside ourselves. Within this zone, we have got used to thinking in a certain way, of feeling in a particular way and of having a specific chemical make up in our blood when expressing our emotions that are only the reflex of a pre-established way of thinking and feeling. There are people who immediately react with rage at the slightest provocation. There are other human beings who experience deep feelings of guilt every time that something painful occurs, even if it's got nothing to do with them. It is important to realize that many of these emotions are nothing more than involuntary patterns of reaction, pure automatic behaviour that we have reinforced over and over again throughout our lives. I'd now like you to imagine that the cells in a human body are continually bombarded with a flood of the hormones related to anger and guilt. The membrane will need to develop a greater number of receptors, of entrance doors, due to the arrival of so many molecules. It is as if the cell itself gets used to this chemical environment and in this way becomes a cell with feelings of guilt and anger. There is no doubt that this can have second effects in the way that the cell works, on the genes that are going to activate themselves and those that are not.

Automatic reactions are not easy to stop because they are not only preferential channels in the brain but also in the cells. That is why particular kinds of stimulus have resonance and great repercussions in every corner of the body.

Fortunately, the cell membrane is plastic and malleable just like the brain circuits. They reproduce themselves and, if they see that the chemical environment in which they live has changed, they will respond with changes in their functioning. I am convinced that physical changes and the healing which you see in many people after changing certain ways of thinking, is a result of this transformation in the cellular response. That is why it is so important to consider the impact of expanding our identity so that it is not so narrow and limited and the effect it can have on our health and vitality.

> "*There are people, for example, who with a few changes in their diet can improve their depressed state [...] People that learn and practice certain breathing methodologies maintain much more positive states of mind than those who do not.*"

When our cells have been submerged into a chemical environment with particular molecules that have been stimulated by emotion, they need to ensure these same molecules remain present in their environment. It is from this moment on that the body demands its "dose", as it were, of a certain hormone and it makes this known to the brain, by means of feeling maps. We are therefore speaking of a form of addiction. We are enclosed in a vicious circle in which a mode of thinking generates some emotions, which in turn means that certain molecules pour into the blood. These, in turn, act on the cells producing certain changes in its membrane. Then, the cell gets used to these changes and demands that the brain, every so often, frees the same kind of substance again. This could also explain why certain changes in our diet, physical exercise and our way of breathing can affect the way in which people think, feel and perceive. All these factors we have just mentioned would have the capacity to alter the chemical environment in which the cell is to be found. This would lead to transformations in the membrane and in the cellular functioning. From this point on, these same cells would demonstrate a resistance to the brain attempting to change the molecules predominating in their environment.

There are people, for example, who with a few changes in their diet can improve their depressed state a considerable amount. Those that do physical exercise on a regular basis know that they are less likely to feel anger or anxiety than those who lead a completely sedentary existence. People that learn and practice certain breathing methodologies maintain much more positive states of mind than those who do not.

Now it is much easier to understand why, when we wish to stop one of these involuntary reactionary patterns of behaviour, we note so much resistance. It is for this reason that we have to develop a great deal of patience in ourselves and with others when speaking of changes.

When you react in a way that you do not like, do not be over critical or judge yourself, as this will not lead you to change. Be compassionate with yourself. Be firm, but not hard. Don't add fuel to the fire. To point an accusing finger at yourself will not make you a better person. Replace shame and guilt with the exercise of responsibility.

14. LEARN TO FORGIVE YOURSELF

"In order for the possible to surface it is necessary to try the impossible over and over again."
HERMANN HESSE

How often have we felt that many of our reactions are far from how we would have liked to have behaved when faced with particular circumstances and situations? After shouting, slamming a door or saying what we never would have wished to say we are generally overcome with feelings of sadness, desperation and even rage at how we have behaved. The voice of our self-criticism echoes over and over again in our heads. We clumsily accept it, perhaps convinced that only by punishing ourselves will we be able to change. Regrettably, the years go by and, quite often, we see that when faced with the same situation, we continue to react in the same way. Just as water ends up eroding stone, the feeling that "everything remains the same" goes on eroding our morale until we come to the conclusion that we can't change.

Many people consciously continue to believe that they can change. Yet when they search a little deeper inside themselves and reflect naturally about how they feel, most of them do not perceive that such a change is actually possible.

What is it that makes it so hard to change certain aspects of our personality? Well, it is that we do not really want to change them, although we think we do. In fact, our involuntary reactions are, as we know, patterns of response that we create when we are of a certain age and a particular level of awareness. We create them to avoid pain and to be able to cover our necessities. These patterns of response are not simply ideas in our heads but authentic neural networks that involve the body. That's why, when we activate these patterns we not only experience a series of particular thoughts but we have a series of feelings and our body responds in a specific way. As we've already seen in a previous chapter, even the cells are connected up in this pattern of response.

There's a beautiful story about a man who was dying. Beside him was his Master, somebody who had acted as his mentor for many years. Thanks to his teachings, he had improved in wisdom and love. He turned a page of his life the moment he met him, as he saw what until that moment had eclipsed him. Despite the fact that (as a consequence of that transformation) the man had been a benefactor for many others, he couldn't manage to shake off a great sadness in his heart, which was weighing on him in these last moments of his life.

"What's wrong?" the master asked him.

"Master, I am overcome with sadness."

"Is it perhaps fear of death?"

"No, Master, I'm not afraid of dying because, thanks to you, I've understood the real nature of death, a veritable rebirth."

"What is it, then, that's bothering you?"

"Master, I can't forgive myself for all the harm I caused before meeting you. Not even all the good I have been able to do all these years I've been at your side can get rid of the clouds of sadness and bitterness in my heart."

The Master then put his disciple into a deep sleep, in which a boy emerged in the middle of a museum. The place was full of works of art of exceptional value: paintings, sculptures, pieces of the most exquisite gold and silver work. In one corner of that museum was a paintbrush, a bucket with black paint and a hammer. The small boy went to the corner, took hold of the paintbrush and the bucket full of paint and began to paint the black paint over the paintings until they were not recognizable. Then he took the hammer and struck the sculptures until they were completely ruined.

Finally, the boy enjoyed seeing how those marvellous pieces of gold and silver work broke into a thousand pieces on falling to the floor. Then, the Master woke his disciple and said to him:

"It is true that the boy in your dream has caused great harm and, yet, the damage has not been caused by his evil but rather through ignorance. If you can, on the one hand, reject his acts and, on the other, forgive him his ignorance, why can't you do the same with yourself?"

In that moment, the disciple understood and, on forgiving himself, he finally was at peace with himself.

We need a big dose of compassion for ourselves in order to come to terms with the suffering that we have caused others and also experienced ourselves. When we understand that neither evil nor the incapacity to do things lies in our hearts but a profound blindness, we will learn to value things from a different perspective. That is why learning to forgive oneself is an essential step to take in order to heal the wounds that lie in our souls.

All these wounds have left a scar in our memories. Today, thanks to scientific research, we know that the memory, with its enormous complexity, does not store only the memory of events that have happened in the past but also sensations, emotions, experiences and adventures.

> **"** *Learning to forgive oneself is an essential step to take in order to heal the wounds that lie in our souls.* **"**

It was our interpretations and value judgements that gave birth to many of the emotions that we feel in any given moment. It is very different to interpreting that somebody doesn't show any love because you are useless than to interpreting that they don't show any love because they really don't know you. That's why, a person who is able to interpret a difficult moment in his life with the light of greater awareness, will alter his past from the present. The past is not something fixed and unchangeable but rather very malleable. If we see it as something fixed and immutable it is because we always see it from the same perspective, using the same parameters.

Maybe seizing hold of our past gives us a solid feeling of identity and yet, we pay a very high price for it. This is, among other reasons, because when we blindly look to our future, it is our past that takes the place of the future. How are we going to aspire to certain ideals and particular horizons if they are hidden from view by the very limited idea that we have of ourselves? It is with ourselves that we have a meeting with destiny and, for this reason, it is our resolutions and our actions that can guide us to one or another place.

Be clear in your mind that
between any event that occurs
and its emotional response
your way of evaluating this
situation will always be there.
It is more important to
interpret things that help us
instead of nullifying us than
to make ostensibly logical
interpretations.

15. THE NECESSARY LESSONS

"Some things we don't understand apprehending them,
but letting them apprehend us."

MOTHER TERESA OF CALCUTTA

It is very usual that when things do not happen as we
would have wished them to, we tend to give ourselves
away, to get frustrated and, above all, to look for the guilty
party or a solution beyond ourselves.

Life is not interested in our personal well-being but
rather that we learn its lessons. So, little by little, we can
show our true potential and we recognize the essence
behind appearances. The phrase, "In life there are no
friends, nor enemies, only masters", invites us to think
that, sometimes, those people we like least are the ones
that have most to teach us about ourselves. They enable
us to recognize, quite often, irritability, impatience and the
lack of compassion that still nestles within us.

Here's a story that can enlighten us about what I've just mentioned.

Close to Paris there was a spiritual community that had been founded by Gurdieff. This man had learned a number of rhythms and dances in diverse monasteries in the desert, which together with another kind of teaching helped people to develop their spirituality. In that community lived an old man that nobody could stand. Known to be unsociable and unfriendly, and despite living among them, the man was not accepted as one of them. One day, this man decided that this place wasn't his home and he left. When Gurdieff heard about this, he went off to look for him until, finally, he found him and tried to convince him to return, to which the man in question roundly refused. Finally, Gurdieff managed to convince him after promising that he would pay him if he went back to live in the community. When the people of that place found out that they not only had to pay Gurdieff to live in that community but now also had to pay so that this despicable individual lived there, they rebelled against that decision. On hearing how his followers had reacted, Gurdieff called them all to a hall and said to them:

"You haven't understood anything. Having a man like this in our community is the greatest gift that I could have

given you. This is because it is the best way for you to learn to develop a compassionate spirit, something that none of you here present have demonstrated to have. Without this spirit, my instructions are worthless to you and, that's why you have to pay me and I have to pay him."

Quite often, realizing some things is sufficiently painful for us that we don't wish to see them. Our brain is much better orientated to avoiding pain than in looking for the compensation and, that is why, when we sense there's going to be suffering we generally stop short and run away. I invite you to try to recall how you felt after bravely facing this cloak of suffering that, without a doubt, has shrouded you on more than one occasion and you'll probably realize that, when you did it, something inside you changed. It was as if you had expanded, as if you had experienced a revolution in your guts. What you did was nothing short of transcending the limits of your identity, your ego, and for this reason you had, even if temporarily, a different experience of reality.

" 'Acceptance' is the impulse to action, to taking on responsibility, to being fully aware that you are indeed capable of responding to whatever happens."

When something happens to us that we don't like, something as simple as missing a plane or that someone rudely interrupts us, we immediately attach a meaning to that event. This meaning has the power to put negative emotions such as rage, frustration or anxiety into play. Overcome with emotion it is very difficult to get away from it if we don't understand the root of what has happened and, that's why, the key word is acceptance, which is nothing more than reconciling oneself with reality. I would like to point out that acceptance has nothing in common with resignation, among other reasons because resignation leads to painful inaction as we consider that there's nothing we can do to change things.

Acceptance achieves what resignation never can as, in contrast to the latter, "acceptance" is the impulse to action, to taking on responsibility, to being fully aware that you are indeed capable of responding to whatever happens. Acceptance implies that the action that you take is not to rebel against what has occurred but rather to rebel against the idea that one has no means of finding a solution.

The moment that I open myself up to the possibility of accepting something, I am also open to the possibility of considering that there may be an opportunity to be found in this situation and that I can look on the other side of the coin, as it were.

On one occasion I was invited to give a conference to a group of about 100 business people in Santiago in Chile who, despite their great personal and professional value, were going through a complex situation due to the huge economic changes that were globally taking place.

The conference had to be given at 9.30 in the morning, the day after I flew from Madrid to Santiago. It was assumed that I would arrive approximately at 10 o'clock at night, after a brief stopover at Buenos Aires Airport. The plane left Madrid and arrived punctually at Buenos Aires and, from there, it took off over night for Santiago, Chile. Just on the point of landing, the pilot told us that, due to a thick fog at Santiago Airport, the plane would have to land in Mendoza. If the truth be told, I couldn't understand the commotion that started up inside the plane. In my ignorance, I thought that Mendoza was located close to Santiago and that there would be no setbacks. It was at this point that I asked the passenger next to me, who with exquisite friendliness explained to me that Mendoza was in Argentina and was on the other side of the Andes Mountains. He also told me that by car it would take about eight hours and that the mountain road left much to be desired. I felt butterflies in my stomach, above all when the plane captain, once we had landed, informed us that the next planes from Mendoza to Santiago would leave the next day at 1.30pm. On hearing this news, the knot tightened, as it seemed impossible that I could be in Santiago at 9.30 in the morning. A great number of passengers began to get irritated and to speak harshly to the air stewardesses, who, besides having been extraordinarily kind during the whole trip, had nothing to do with what had happened as they were simply doing their job. This shows you how irrational people can be.

When I got off the plane I spoke with the airport staff and nobody gave me any alternative, at least for my purposes. I was exhausted after such a long journey and I couldn't see myself driving a car for eight hours in the middle of the Andes. It was just then that I realized that I wasn't accepting the situation. I wasn't reconciling myself with reality but rebelling against it which, in turn, was stirring up the emotions which I was least craving, emotions like frustration or desperation. It was in that precise moment when I radically changed my attitude. I couldn't alter what was happening to me but I could change my response. It was then that I began to say to myself that there had to be an opportunity hidden in this apparent problem and if I persevered I would find it. What I first noticed was a great change in my emotional state.

From feeling frustrated I began to feel interested and, little by little, hopeful in discovering something valuable that, in that moment, was hidden from my view. Desperation became confidence that I would find a way, although at that moment, I couldn't see it. Suddenly I became aware of something that was so obvious that I'd forgotten it and that was the fact that my conference speech had no other title than, "Human Potential Faced with Uncertainty". I knew that the unexplored talent of people is only revealed when we are outside our comfort area and we find ourselves faced with the unknown. Once again it was a wonderful occasion to pass from teacher to student and that made me feel enthusiasm in the face of whatever came my way.

One of the things that had most saddened me before starting the journey from Madrid to Santiago in Chile was that, I would both go there and return at night and I wouldn't be able to contemplate the beautiful spectacle of the Andes.

Thanks to the unconditional help of the organization that had invited me to give the conference, they organized a system of transport so that I would be picked up at Mendoza, would change car at the Argentinian frontier and the other car would take me from there to Santiago. I travelled all night with two drivers who both had a great sense of humour and were incredibly friendly so that I hardly noticed the trip. Besides I was in an ecstatic state contemplating dawn over the Andes Mountain range and I arrived at 9 o'clock exactly, just half an hour before the conference was due to begin. I had also had such a good time and had enjoyed so much seeing the Andes that I entered the conference hall with explosive energy which was of great use in giving my conference talk and in connecting with the audience.

That's why, although it takes more or less time to apply it, I try never to forget that the best options for allowing the door of opportunity to be opened are in not allowing myself to get trapped in automatic reactions, however logical or reasonable they may seem. The best opportunity lies in asking myself, "What could be of value in what is happening to me?"

Helen Keller, the woman who, despite becoming blind, deaf and dumb whilst a girl, graduated with honours at Radcliff, stated, "If you stare at the sun, you won't see the darkness."

There's another element that can help us very much to reduce the stress in our lives. I am referring to gratitude and I'd like to illustrate what I am talking about by telling another story.

A man went to the doctor's because of a number of unknown pains that he had been having.

"Yes, doctor, I am really fed up; all my body is in pain. Everything in my life is going badly. It's a complete mess."

The doctor began to get the feeling that, perhaps, there was a certain relationship between his physical pain and his emotional pain because the man kept complaining about how bad his life was and how horrible things in general were. So, as he knew some of his family and personal background, he said to him, "I understand perfectly and, besides, you just can't imagine how sad I am about the death of your wife."

The man looked at him, perplexed.

"But, doctor, my wife is in fine shape; someone must have informed you wrongly."

"You just can't know how happy I am that your wife is fine."

Then he wrote on a sheet of paper, while saying out loud: "His wife is alive."

"By the way," the doctor continued, "I'm sorry that one of your sons is sick."

"But, doctor, how strange you are today; my sons, fortunately, are all healthy."

"His sons are healthy," the doctor commented while writing it down.

"I don't wish to deepen your wound, but I am sorry that you've lost your job."

"Doctor, I don't understand what's wrong with you, but..."

And in that moment the man understood the little he had valued all the good things in his life and how he'd been overcome by some feelings that could only have their origin in a very partial vision of things. Then, he got up, thanked the doctor and left.

It doesn't make sense that we wear ourselves out wishing to change things that, right from the start, are outside our reach. I refer to conflicts or problems at a global level and feeling we are unable to manage our own states of mind. Saying yes to life has much to do with ceasing to adopt the role of victims, dedicating our valuable time and energy to search for the guilty party and in being responsible the moment we respond to what has happened to us.

A FINAL WORD

Facing resistance and resignation we have acceptance and gratitude. Maybe because neither acceptance nor gratitude seems real options we allow ourselves to be overcome with the idea that neither seems possible.

16. FROM DARKNESS TO LIGHT

"You don't enter the system to see if it works because if you are in the system you can't be outside it."

BARBARA KENT

One of the novels I've always found most enjoyable is The Count of Montechrist by Alexander Dumas. It's a story with secrets, intrigue and envy that leads a young man called Edmund Dantés, in the flower of his youth, in love and with a promising future, to be imprisoned for 16 years in the castle of If. This high-security prison was located on an island facing the French city of Marseille. Deprived of his freedom, and without understanding the strange circumstances by which he had ended up there, he lives in a state of confusion, bitterness and loneliness. It is not until he meets another prisoner, the abbey Faria, that he starts to understand the bizarre chain of events which led to his imprisonment. Edmund Dantés discovers the betrayal brought on by the jealousy of some of his companions. He also gets to know a secret of such characteristics, which if it were made public, would lead to the imprisonment of one of the most important politicians in France.

We often call a comfortable life a life of simple resignation. The difference between us and Edmund Dantés is that he knew that behind those walls was another, much more beautiful reality, while we don't. That's why, the walls of the mind are more solid than the walls of stone as they have the capacity not even to contemplate the possibility that another reality different from the one we know is possible.

When in our lives something happens that we don't like such as not being acknowledged or thanked, or perhaps we come across a person who refuses to collaborate with us, we immediately reject that person or situation. This is very sensible and reasonable, and that's precisely the problem. We choose things with our heart and we use reason to justify them and in the end what we decide to feel will immediately be backed up by solid logical arguments.

There is a curious character in the Sufi world called Mullah Nasruddin, known for being both a sage and an eccentric. One day, Nasruddin was dropping breadcrumbs around him, when a neighbour came up to him and asked him, "What are you doing, Nasruddin?"

"I'm trying to keep the tigers at bay," responded Nasruddin.

"But there are no tigers for thousands of kilometres around here," the perplexed neighbour replied.

"A clear demonstration of the efficiency of my method, don't you think?" responded Nasruddin.

The world that seems reasonable to us is not the world of logic but the world of automatisms. That's why, it is only reasonable that we get tense and angry when faced with stimuli that generate a lack of comfort. The world of the reasonable seems so irresistibly logical that we clutch at it as if it were the only one possible. This is why when we look at ourselves we find reasons, proof and justifications that reinforce the idea that we are in the right and the other person, wrong.

We've already seen in other chapters that, when one has created a number of mental filters, all or nearly all the invitations that reality presents us with, to go beyond those filters, are rejected and we are not even aware of them. Nevertheless, I'd like to ask you a series of questions:

- **Why is it that when someone driving hoots their horn for no good reason and we hoot back, our blood pressure rises?**

- **Why does our stomach turn when we see somebody who we dislike in the street?**

- **Why is it that, after an argument, we get so tired and we have a headache?**

- **Why is it that when we don't feel fairly treated, it is difficult for us to get to sleep?**

If all our emotional responses make such sense, why doesn't the body remain calm and balanced? Shouldn't the head and the rest of the body all act together?

> " *Reactions such as rage [...], when they are prolonged in time and cease to be emotions and become states of mind, have very adverse effects.* "

As we have seen and I believe it is beneficial to remind ourselves, reactions like rage, resentment, revenge, frustration, desperation, lack of trust, anxiety and anguish, when they are prolonged in time and cease to be emotions and become states of mind, have very adverse effects:

- **They harm our health and vitality, damaging our immune systems, arteries, heart, muscles and viscera.**

- **They generate alienation amongst people, destroying families, friendships, towns and whole countries.**

- **They block out the motivation to create prosperity.**

- They reduce and even wipe out mental clarity and any kind of possibility to see things with a certain perspective, killing the entrepreneur spirit.

- They become an obstacle to the possibility of knowing, discovering, understanding and learning.

If these emotions spontaneously came into play with something we brand as undesirable, thus causing negative effects, it wouldn't be such a bad idea to consider whether we are left with any other option.

Obviously, we are not going to find this alternative option with the intellect because it is from there that the problem germinates. The option comes from the world of our being, our consciousness. It comes from the reality that we already are but that we have neglected.

In order for us to move on this plane we need to go through a series of levels, which is going to demand of us a firm compromise, a great deal of stamina and a lot of patience.

First level: No event or circumstance, however reasonable it may seem to me, can give rise to harbouring negative thoughts inside myself which, in turn, trigger dysfunctional emotions. For this reason, whenever I notice that I am beginning to harbour some of these thoughts or to feel some of these emotions, I must first pause, breathe deeply three or four times and avoid, as far as possible, these thoughts or emotions gripping me again. Bear in mind that this process is arduous. Firstly, because we are trying to stop automatisms that have been reinforced over many years. Secondly, because our intellectual minds (which is part of the problem) is going to tell us that what we are doing is completely idiotic and a great waste of time.

Second level: Accept this situation, not as a load, but as a gift of the Universe so that we can create and develop in peace, compassion and love.

Third level: At this level we have to have great humility, opening ourselves up to the possibility that behind what we now see and feel there is a new space, a space where joy and an enormous clarity is to be found. That's why faith and confidence, that behind the walls of the mind another reality exists (which we are blinded to now), are so important.

Fourth level: On getting to this point, we need to direct our attention in a very different way, to the way the automatisms lead us. When we feel that someone has injured us, immediately our attention dedicates itself to the search for everything negative, disagreeable and dysfunctional in that individual. If we wish to transcend our automatisms and be truly free, it is important that we begin to look for the best in that person, as there is something admirable in every human being. What we are really looking for is not to get obsessed with the appearance or behaviour of that person but in his or her essence. We need to see what there is behind those wounds and emotional fractures and what the source of their pain is.

Fifth level: This is a level that shocks our habitual level of pride, of wishing to do everything ourselves and without help. There are forces that we can't understand with reasoning and that science is only beginning to understand. This is the fifth level and we ask the Universe for help, so that it can help us in relation to ourselves and others.

Quite a few years ago I was in London studying certain aspects of the human mind. One day, by chance, I found out that in one of the city museums they were exhibiting a series of anatomical models from the 17th century that came from Italy and were made of wax. When I went, I couldn't believe how real those figures seemed. You could follow each blood vessel (arterious, venous and lymphatic) with the greatest of detail. There were models of organs by themselves as well as entire bodies. I, who am in love with human anatomy, enjoyed myself enormously. Suddenly, I realized that about ten metres from where I stood, was a kind of arc and, beyond that, what seemed to be the skulls of animals. I decided to go into that small room and, effectively, I saw on one of the walls, on a small shelf, some wolf skulls. I had already seen that on my left, on one of the walls was drawn a beautiful image of the anatomical amphitheatre of Padua. In the Papua Amphitheatre some of the most prestigious anatomists of the epoch learned their trade, like the great Vesalio. Without a doubt, it became the most famous amphitheatre in the whole world.

What I hadn't noticed was that, to my right, just by the opposite wall to the image of the Padua Amphitheatre was a bench where a boy of about 18 was sitting. Completely oblivious to this fact, on my part, I was obstructing his view of the Padua Amphitheatre, as I was standing in the middle.

He shouted at me to get out of the way in such a way that a lady who was also looking at the skulls began to tremble. The first thing I noticed was that I felt stress throughout my body and a rapid increase in my heart and breathing rate. I was aware of the force with which my jaw contracted and the rage I felt towards that person who had treated me in such an aggressive way. I looked at him enraged and perceived all that was ugly in him for some seconds. Suddenly, as if struck by a ray of light, I became fully aware that I had an option, the option to forgive and so I did this in my deepest self. I can testify what then happened because I am aware of what I had experienced. On making that choice all the tension in my body disappeared completely in a split second. My jaw relaxed, my heart and breathing became calm and I was overcome with a deep state of serenity and calm.

As a doctor, all these experiences leave me perplexed, because I know about the great hormonal, muscular and visceral changes that take place with a discharge of rage and just how hard it is, even with medication, to reduce the blood pressure or simple muscular tension. That a simple choice, that of not looking for reasons and justifications for counter-attacking, can have the capacity to bring everything back into focus in just a moment, even experiencing it as I had, remains difficult to believe. Nevertheless, what had the greatest impact on me was not this but when I looked at this young man again, I saw something that I hadn't seen before and in some way I understood the suffering that he must have had in order to react in that way. My rage turned to compassion, which is not the same as pity, as compassion implies a bonding with the suffering of the other person.

Perhaps the young man had felt ignored or scorned by me and that may have activated some painful memories. But I consider my lack of reaction had some impact on the young man, as he now seemed to be calmer and more relaxed.

*That day I learned something very important, that,
with relative success, I try to apply every day. I became
aware that you don't put out fire with petrol, but with
water. This means stopping the involuntary reaction
however reasonable it seems and choosing who you want to
be in any given moment.*

I know that we tend to think that the key to everything
is "to do" so as "to have" and later "to be": carrying out
various actions to possess certain things which in turn allow
us to be recognized, prestigious and happy. I believe that this
is not a healthy paradigm and that, perhaps, we could invert
it. When the first thing one looks for is to be, to do is in
keeping with this being and this is what gives rise to having.
Only from a balanced, true, complete and compassionate
self can actions be born that are so essentially so different
that they end up forming new realities. It is our level of
awareness that determines our level of self. An ordinary
consciousness is on the plane of what is reasonable, and so,
we do what it is logical to do and we get what it is sensible
to get. When you enter this other level of consciousness,
you do what you do not because you have reasons. You
choose this path and for that reason you get something both
extraordinary and unexpected.

A FINAL WORD

When we work to act not based
on our emotions but on our
choices, this is when we act
in freedom.

17. RETURNING HOME

"It doesn't worry me how something will be resolved because I remain curious, fascinated and hopeful about what can begin to emerge."

DR. MILTON ERICKSON

Our identity, as we have already seen on numerous occasions, bombards us with a never-ending series of thoughts; it generates such mental noise that we are not able to hear the much more subtle sound of that hidden dimension that we know as "being", "essence" or "witness".

About 2,500 years ago, in India, a number of authentic scientists made an incredible discovery. They unravelled one of mankind's most surprising mysteries: the way in which the human mind works. Only recently has the most advanced medicine been capable of understanding (at least partially) what is the physiological explanation to some of the effects that practitioners of what is known today as mindfulness, experience.

What the practitioners of mindfulness look for is nothing less than to reduce the mental noise, so that, little by little, the essence that makes up who we really are becomes clearer and more palpable. Listening to it is penetrating into a dimension from which springs an extraordinary flow of energy, vitality, wisdom and creativity.

We are all so used to going over things again and again in our heads that training ourselves to cease this incessant dialogue makes us feel disturbed and exposed. We have the feeling that in the emptiness and silence nothing exists and, that's why, we feel it is absurd to spend part of our precious time developing the capacity to stop our thoughts and remain in silence.

This is one of the greatest doubts that might come to mind because it implies a radical exit from our comfort zone, our familiar neighbourhood.

Most of us generally live with enormous mental stress. This mental stress manifests itself as anxiety, anguish and different kinds of mental blocks, greatly lowering our capacity for clear-thinking, taking decisions and learning. We know that the cause of this is the setting off of the alarm system in our body or our sympathetic nervous system through thinking.

One of the most fascinating discoveries that have occurred in the world of medicine in relation to the meditation technique, mindfulness, is that when the incessant mental noise caused by the hyperactivated sympathetic nervous system stops, the body responds very favourably. The first thing one appreciates is a relaxation of the muscles and a better working digestive apparatus. The blood pressure drops and so does the cholesterol level. The metabolism, which reflects the energy consumption of our organism, is lowered so that the person experiences an increase in energy and vitality as the energy ceases to be used up in other less productive ways. The heart also benefits as it has to work with less resistance, and this in turn reduces its oxygen needs. Along with this, there is a significant improvement in the immune system and in the organism's defence system, especially in regard to the lymphocytes NK and CD4. This means a reduction in the possibility of developing an infection or tumour.

It is surprising how neuroimaging studies which use functional magnetic resonance show that people who have trained in meditation have a thicker left pre-frontal cortex. Remember that this area does not only have a great impact on the spreading and activation of the nervous system for recovery or parasympathetic, but also is a key player when coming to experience positive emotions like joy, enthusiasm and serenity. That is one of the reasons why the study and the practice of mindfulness meditation is getting more and more popular in a society that puts up with very high levels of stress which is made manifest in the growth of the number of people suffering anxiety and its consequent depression.

Both do not only affect our productive output but also generate insomnia and greatly increase the chances of having a road accident.

> *"One of the most efficient systems for keeping your attention centred on the here and now is [...] to pay attention to our breathing movements, as breathing takes place in the present."*

Once we have understood the way that mindfulness meditation works, we need to understand what the basic methodology of its practice is.

Given that disturbing thoughts cannot exist if we do not pay any attention to them, the key to everything is to gain back control of our attention. This kind of meditation also invites us to remain locked in the here and now without letting our mind travel to the past or future. If you close your eyes and try to keep thinking in the present without getting overcome by thoughts from the past or ideas about what you're going to do in the future, you will feel the benefits of mindfulness meditation, as others have. If this is very difficult for you, don't worry as this is quite normal and it happens to most of us. That's why it requires training.

One of the most efficient systems for keeping your attention centred on the here and now is, as we saw in a previous chapter, to pay attention to our breathing movements, as breathing takes place in the present.

Another of the essential elements to take into account is how we react to distractions. When, all of a sudden, we realize that we have stopped paying attention to our breathing and have become totally wrapped up in a thought or emotion, the key is not to get angry but to gently and firmly bring one's attention back to our breathing. One might compare this to bringing a puppy we are training back to our side after sniffing at a flower. This is an essential point, as one cannot experience meditation if we don't abandon this tendency we have to feel bad or guilty every time we get distracted.

The next element, and perhaps the trickiest, is what to do when an emotion is so intense or a thought is so persistent that we feel it is impossible not to get involved with it. However hard we try, we only manage to return our attention to our respiration for a few seconds, to then only return quickly to that thought or emotion. In this case what we have to do is simply focus on the corporal sensations that this thought or emotion produces in us. It is also useful to give this experience a name: "sadness", "fear" or "anxiety". The key point here is not to fight it, as the use of force or willpower is counter-productive. What we need to do to free ourselves of this situation is to let ourselves go with the flow, like we would on contemplating a wonderful landscape. Do not reject the thought or the emotion as bad or undesirable. Live it fully without passing judgement. Become an explorer who is trying to find the profound source to what he is going through. Little by little, the thought or emotion will disappear or it will reveal something of great value that had been hidden from you beforehand.

The type of meditation called mindfulness doesn't have a place for categorizing thoughts or emotions as good or bad, desirable or not, as we have to suspend judgement completely. What we find in mindfulness meditation is an attitude of exploration, which shows the same interest in studying an exotic garden or an arid desert. This attitude is fundamental and is in direct opposition to the way that our mind generally works; which immediately sticks to what it likes and resists or rejects what it dislikes.

Mindfulness meditation is one of the most interesting ways to enter this magical arena which is our essential self, transcending the boundaries of our own identity. The practice of it is not searching for a rational understanding (an intellectual understanding of what occurs), but in fully living an experience, opening up to the possibilities and potential that we have inside ourselves. For this reason, any attempt to achieve or feel something is very counter-productive.

Mindfulness meditation invites us to let go of our tendency to be in control of everything and to want to understand everything that happens to us intellectually.

It is an invitation to have faith and to go with the flow of wisdom that challenges any understanding on the part of our narrow, blind identity. Mindfulness meditation is a path towards widening our personal perspectives, development and growth. It is a path that leads us from what seems reasonable to what is truly possible.

Silence is not the absence of
sound but noise. Only when
we stop the rushing stream of
thoughts that assails us, can we
hear that voice that comes not
from the head but from
the heart.

18. THE DARK NIGHT OF THE SOUL

" If a man conquered a thousand men a thousand times
in a battle, and another conquered only one, himself, then
that man would really be the greater of the conquerors."

EL DHAMMAPADA

Many mystics, on their path to find God, have
mentioned a period of confusion, sadness, fear
and solitude which they've named, "the dark night of the
soul". Many of us, despite not being mystics, also have the
sensation that, when we wish to abandon the space that
we have call "identity" we enter into another full of doubt
and confusion. In this new area which is also known
as "the breakdown zone", a human being feels lost and
finds it difficult to think clearly. Everything around him
is covered in mist and he doesn't know where to go from
here. Anxiety, fear and desperation come to the surface.
The judging mind, whose only objective for us is, like a
sheep, to return to the flock, starts to bombard us with

interpretations and value judgements that only encourage us to give up exploring and return to our starting point. Then we usually feel we should never have left that starting point in the first place. It is a wake-up call to resignation, conformity, to a belief that personal change is only a beautiful utopia.

We have to be very alert when we begin to go through that dark night because, in reality, what is happening is actually the opposite of what it appears. If we abandon the path in this moment and are guided once again by our emotions, then we will undoubtedly lose much of what we had gained by daring to leave our comfort zone. When we feel lost and confused it is because we are on the verge of making a discovery, of having a revelation. This is because behind this dark area where we sink there is an area of discovery, the place where one begins to get a deep understanding of certain things. This is the place where our creativity is awoken and we find new paths to enter that place which before (when we were in our comfort zone) we had put off entering.

We don't only need to have the true heart of a warrior in order to leave the comfort zone, but we also need to have that same spirit to continue going forward in the midst of all the confusion and darkness. It is essential to keep up one's courage, confidence and absolute belief that something of value (although now hidden) is germinating within ourselves. Our consciousness has woken up but our intellectual and rational mind, dependent on our ego, doesn't know what is happening but whatever it is, in some way it knows that it is threatening its existence. This reaction of our identity (our ego) is normal as when the real awakening of our consciousness begins, the ego won't die but will simply start to vanish. It will be a bit like when the darkness disappears in the presence of light.

If we feel bad when we are traversing our dark night it is not because we are sick, but rather because we are so used to believing that we are just our identity, that we experience its emotions while it is being transformed, as our own emotions. Just like the caterpillar in the phase of being a chrysalis has to be digested by its own protolithic enzymes in order to transform into a butterfly, our identity has to be digested so that a new being much more in line with whom we really are, emerges.

> **"**When our consciousness ceases to identify itself with our identity (with that definition we have made of ourselves), we immediately gain access to new possibilities for ourselves and our lives.**"**

To fight these new emotions we are experiencing is just the opposite of what we should do. If we resist we reject and oppose that which is most crucial to us. To embrace these uncomfortable emotions may not seem sensible, but nevertheless, from the point of view of a higher consciousness, it is just what we need to do if we wish to grow and evolve as humans.

It is in these precise moments that we have to be firm, to carry on and accept our feelings. We need to be open to experience things fully, giving in to the curing process that is so necessary for us. In these moments of pain and bitterness, rays of joy and enthusiasm can appear. When we understand that behind the confusion comes light and that after the darkest night we will see the most beautiful sunrise. If we manage to escape from that mirage created by the emotions which are unfortunately at the service of our narrow selves and our limited consciousness, we will have immediate access to new possibilities for ourselves and our lives. In other words, when our consciousness ceases to identify itself with our identity (with that definition we have made of ourselves), we immediately gain access to new possibilities for ourselves and our lives. It is comparable with seeing things from a higher viewpoint from where we can see what is unseen from ground level.

The search for oneself (for who we really are) is always a heroic act that involves learning to overcome oneself many times, in order to expand the limits of our own identity bit by bit. Only in this way can we get to discover the extraordinary within the ordinary. Einstein himself stated that, "in life, either nothing is a miracle or everything is a miracle." There are hidden dimensions to reality that will only be made manifest once we have been through our dark night of the soul. Our senses then will be able to pick up elements of that reality that was hidden from view by our judging mind.

> **"** *The moment we feel lost, confused and frustrated, it is essential that we actively collaborate in the process of transformation.* **"**

This is a good moment to remember the words pronounced by Nelson Mandela and written down by Marianne Williamson, where he said that man is not afraid of his dark side but of his light.

The moment we feel lost, confused and frustrated, it is essential that we actively collaborate in the process of transformation, and to this end there are several things that we can do, because all of them have an impact on our emotions.

- **Maintain a posture and gestures that shows clearly we are going through a victorious process and not a defeat. Sagging shoulders, a bent back and**

the chest contracted are all signs read
by the brain as if something bad was
taking place and they reinforce the
dysfunctional emotions. The same thing
happens with sad faces and a weak tone
of voice. So move with energy, speak with
enthusiasm and transmit passion with
your eyes.

- Sleep at least seven hours daily so that
during sleep, our subconscious can carry
on working bringing to light what has to
come to light.

- Try to eat moderately and prepare
light suppers.

- Break the sedentary habit and do
physical exercise at least five days a week,
for half an hour every day. Physical
exercise has, as we've already seen,
the capacity to reduce many of our
dysfunctional emotions.

- Practice mindfulness meditation for ten
minutes twice a day, reaching 20 minutes
twice a day little by little.

- Appreciate what is happening to us in the way I have explained earlier, as a great opportunity for our growth and development.
- Don't waste time asking questions such as, "Why do I feel so bad?", "What can I do to feel better?", "What is the cause of how I feel?" These questions are tricks so that we get involved with our emotions and get trapped by them. Different questions like, "What is wonderful about what I'm going through?", "How can I get even more involved in my process of transformation?", or "What will I discover that is extraordinary?" These questions make our attention focus on the search for the way out. They do not remain shrouded in a series of reflections that don't lead us anywhere and only keep us trapped.

Any process of transformation takes a different amount of time in each human being and takes place when we least expect it to. The only thing that we can do is mark off the path and await victory. That's how we'll be victorious.

A FINAL WORD

If we wish to feel more energy
and vitality, we need to bear in
mind all our dimensions: the
cognitive, affective, corporal
and spiritual as they are all
inter-connected.

19. A NEW LIFE

"In the search of wisdom, every day you obtain something.
In the search for TAO, every day you leave something
behind."

LAO-TSU

When, little by little, we start to transcend our self
(our ego), we begin to have a completely different
experience of ourselves and reality. There is a metaphor
widely applied describing this process. Try to imagine
that during your whole life you've believed that you were
the character in a movie. The movie is of life as it is
normally lived, with its moments of joy and its moments
of great sadness.

Now, imagine for a moment that you suddenly realized
that you were, in fact, none of the characters in that movie
but a spectator inside a cinema. Although it is true you can
laugh and cry at what happens to the characters, you know
that none of them are you. When we get wrapped up in one

of the characters of the film, we believe that we are that and nothing more than that. This is to fully identify with our personality. Nevertheless, when we realize that in reality we are a spectator watching the movie, we are then identifying with our true essence, with what we really are. This is the plane of being: we have transcended the character and we have found our true nature which is of a spiritual kind. Distanced from the drama in this way, enables us to maintain our serenity and level-headedness whatever we see on the screen. That is why there are people when faced with very traumatic circumstances do not lose their composure or peace of mind.

The possibilities that open up to us when we awake to our true nature are multiple:

First: From this dimension, one experiences pain, but not suffering. There is pain when there is loss, but one does not think continually about this event until the point that it ruins his or her life.

Second: In the new dimension there is an emotional detachment that means the following: one can feel the emotion but without getting trapped by it.

Third: In the new dimension there is a different perception of reality and you see many things that before were hidden and you hear things that before you couldn't hear.

Fourth: In the new dimension you can see how deeply interconnected everything is and the illusion of separation disappears. In some way I discover that the harm that I do to others turns against me and that the harm I do to the Earth I am doing to myself.

Fifth: In the new dimension you take a step further than what Einstein showed us. In the new Earth the illusion of time disappears and there is only a never-ending present, only the here and now.

Sixth: In the new dimension there is an unruffled sense of calm and peace, even when on the plane of our identity we are going through very difficult circumstances.

Seventh: In the new dimension there is freedom of choice because one has transcended one's habits, one's involuntary reactions, one's automatisms, one's everyday modes of response.

Eighth: In the new dimension you have the clarity to understand the suffering caused by living trapped on the plane of the identity. For this reason, not only do you have a profound compassion, implying an understanding of the suffering of others and the source of their behaviour, but you also have the capacity to forgive way beyond what you could from the plane of identity.

Ninth: In the ninth dimension no language exists. This is why those that have glimpsed this new Earth or habitually live on it, can orientate, explain and describe things but they can't transmit by means of language the experience of being there.

Tenth: In the new dimension one experiences unconditional love because from this angle you can only perceive the beauty in others although it is understood that on the plane of the identity this beauty is very often covered by cloaks of ugliness.

Eleventh: In the new dimension forms do not exist. Nevertheless you can acquire the ability of creating and manifesting all kinds of form on the plane of reality where our identity is.

Twelfth: In the new dimension there is an extraordinarily high level of intelligence and wisdom and, for this reason, there is an incredible clarity which is not to be had on the plane of identity.

When a person ceases fully identifying himself with his mind, with his thoughts, judgements, opinions and emotions he will then understand that he is much more than his ideas and opinions. Then he'll begin to understand what there is behind the words, "I am".

Buddhism also has much to teach us and there is a very interesting story about what happened to the prince Gautama Siddhartha when he penetrated this new dimension whilst meditating by a tree in Nepal. It appears that, after waking up to this new reality, to this new Earth, he began to walk when he found a man walking in the opposite direction. Siddhartha must have had an extraordinary appearance or look on his face for that man walking to stop short and ask him:

"Who are you, a god?"

Siddhartha replied, "I am the Buddha."

The translation of these words is none other than, "I am the one who is awake".

To my mind, no-one in history has shown in such a surprising and beautiful way what it is to be human and, at the same time, be on another plane of reality, as Jesus of Nazareth. He continually reminded us that there was another kingdom, another dimension on which we could live. He was harshly judged and punished by the people that lived tied to their egos and who were, therefore, incapable of accepting something even though their eyes could contemplate it.

In some ways, when we move on the plane of identity and the ego, in order to be able to understand something that happens and that we aren't able to comprehend, we have to find an explanation that enables us to adapt the magnitude of the event to our narrow-mindedness. Barbaric actions have been taken by people in our attempt to adapt reality to the measure of our meagre minds.

When a person begins to enter this new dimension (that of the Spirit) all the expressiveness of that individual (his face, his look) acquire a new quality and even the most simple action is transformed not only in what he does, but above all and fundamentally in how he does it.

It is difficult to understand how 2,000 years ago, a few plain fishermen left their boats, nets, jobs and even their families to follow someone who dressed so simply and they didn't even know. It is difficult to understand how someone can follow another person who says to you that you are going to be "fishermen of souls". However, something in Jesus' eyes, in his presence, in his tone of voice, moved their hearts in such a way that they did something illogical, which was neither sensible nor reasonable. Many people in the world today are Christians thanks to those disciples that leaped from the reasonable to the possible. Today, thanks to those human beings without any academic schooling, many people like myself (who have been fortunate to have had access to academic studies) have realized that no studying, no intellectual knowledge, can lead us to what is a new dimension of reality.

When the spirit dimension becomes reality in our consciousness, the world not made manifest, the world without form will begin to transform our personality. All this has enormous repercussions. Not only in how our mental processes function but also in how this affects our body. I am convinced that many healings which are not understood by medical science are related to the intervention of this new dimension from which new possibilities emerge and can create new realities.

0Dear reader, many thanks for coming with me on this inward journey into the human being. I would like to part company with a question which invites you to continue exploring all this beauty, this wisdom and this force that exists within us: Is it the miracle which gives rise to the believer or is it the believer who gives rise to the miracle? Forever yours.

ACKNOWLEDGEMENTS

*I would like to thank a number of people who gave their time,
their advice and their great love.*

To María Benjumea, President of Infoempleo, for being for me, a real leader, someone
who constantly tries to get the best out of people. She shows us with her joy, enthusiasm
and confidence that true leaders are those that help to create ties and to demolish walls.
Thanks also for reading the original manuscript and for giving
me such valuable ideas on to how to improve it.
To Jaime Antoñanzas, a greatly-loved friend and for me an example of intelligence,
friendliness, generosity and creativity. To him I owe many of the best
remedies that have come to fruition in this book.
To my great friends at Comunica+A. To Pablo, Javier and Alfonso
Antoñanzas, for their love, for their exceptional ideas and for their help.
To Jordi Nadal, my Publisher, a great friend and a person who knows how to dream up
great ideas and chase his dreams with such enthusiasm and
determination that they become exceptional realities.
To all the staff at Plataforma Editorial, for their incredible
dedication and help in making this book.
To the members of HSM, the company that organizes my conferences
in Spain so efficiently and professionally.
To those in charge of Izi Palestras, Cristina Santiago and Liliana Padura,
for their affection and for their exceptional work.
To all those people that give me the opportunity to collaborate as a professor
in their prestigious universities and training centres.
To all the staff at EBS, and especially to Carlos Ongallo, Israel Jorge and Raúl de Tena.
To all those professional people that work in the Centro Europeo de Estudios y
Formación Empresarial Garrigues and in particular its director, Ángel Bizcarrondo.
To all the staff at Instituto de Empresa and especially to Cuqui Cabanas and Pilar Rojo.
To all the people that form part of IDDI, part of the University
Francisco of Vitoria, and especially the university rector, Daniel Sada, the director
of IDDI, Natalia Márquez, and to course director, Susana Alonso.
To the members of Euroforum Escorial. To the members of Deusto Business
School and especially to Víctor Urcelay.
To my dear friend Eugenio Palomero and to all the members of Itiníribus.
To the Asociación para el Progreso de la Dirección and particularly
to María Arrien, Enrique Sánchez de León and Ignacio Pausa.
To Alberto Saiz, Álex Rovira, Fernando Trías de Bes, Juan Carlos Cubeiro, Ovidio
Peñalver, Pilar Jericó, Juan Mateo, José Ballesteros, Javier Fernández Aguado, Ignacio
Martínez Mendizábel, Daniel Romero Abreu and so many other friends
with whom I have spent such special moments.
To my good friends at the Grupo Hospital de Madrid.
To all my patients and the participants on my courses, for their warmth and trust.